WORD PLAY
ENGAGING ACTIVITIES THAT TEACH HOW WORDS WORK
GRADES 5-6

BY MARY ROSENBERG

CARSON-DELLOSA PUBLISHING COMPANY, INC.
GREENSBORO, NORTH CAROLINA

Editor
Sabena Maiden

Layout Design
Sharon Thompson
Jon Nawrocik

Inside Illustrations
Mike Duggins

Cover Design
Peggy Jackson

Cover Photo
© Brand X Pictures

TABLE OF CONTENTS

INTRODUCTION

Word Play encourages students to have fun playing with words while learning how letters can be changed and manipulated to make the words they say and write each day, as well as builds their vocabulary of new words. The variety of activities in this book involve making words by changing or rearranging the letters used in different words. While students play with a word, they are actually doing challenging "word work."

The illustrations in *Word Play* serve an important role by providing extra support to students who may have had little experience in spelling, reading, and working with words. By looking at the illustrations, students are either given some hints as to what needs to be done in the word activities or are better able to understand some of the words that need to be made.

The activities in *Word Play* are perfect for:
- whole-class instruction to introduce word concepts.
- homework assignments for reinforcement.
- word-center activities.
- partner and small-group work.
- individual student review.
- take-home activities for students to complete with parents.

Ways to Use the Activities

The activities in *Word Play* can be used in many different ways. Some suggestions are:
- Make copies of a specific word-play section and assemble the pages into individual packets for students needing review or reinforcement of particular word concepts.

- Make copies of select pages and staple or bind them into individual books for students. Have each student keep a book in her desk and assign the activities as needed.

- Make a transparency of a particular page and make a copy of the page for each student for whole-class instruction.

Descriptions of Activities and Extension Ideas

Below is a brief description of each word activity, as well as ideas for extending the concepts and skills presented in *Word Play*. Most of the activities in this book can be easily extended by integrating a classroom spelling list, new vocabulary list, student names, or key terms from any curricular unit.

Stepping Out (pages 9-16)

In this word-building activity, students make longer words by adding one letter to the base word shown on the first rung until the top of each ladder is reached. Letters can be inserted between other letters, but their order cannot be changed. The top of each ladder contains a goal word for students to make.

Extension idea: Have students use copies of the reproducible on page 118 to complete their own word-ladder activities to share with the class or to take home. As a class, have students design a large word-building activity to be placed on a wall or bulletin board using different graphics, such as train cars or caterpillar sections.

What's in the Middle? (pages 17-26)

In this compound word activity, students find the middle word that serves as a connection for the first and last words in each set.

Extension idea: To extend this activity, have students brainstorm other compound words. Record the compound words on index cards, writing the first word segment on one card and the second segment on another. Have the class use the cards to create new, interactive "What's in the Middle?" activities. This activity is great for placing in a word center.

Hidden Words (pages 27-34)

In this word-parts activity, students insert short words to complete longer words that can be grouped in particular categories, such as holidays or people.

Extension idea: To extend this activity, provide students with a list of words, such as the current spelling list. Have students look for words hiding within larger words, then type or neatly write each word on paper. Have students use different-colored markers to highlight each short word within the larger words.

What's in Common? (pages 35-42)
In this word-category activity, students sort words into different groups. This activity is a challenge since some words could be placed in more than one category. Since each word can only be used once, advise students to think and choose carefully when placing each word in its category.

Extension idea: Create a class "What's in Common?" activity. Have students brainstorm various topics. Then, announce six topics and have each student select three words that fit with each topic. Allow students to share their answers to see the similarities and differences among their answers.

In Other Words (pages 43-50)
In this making-words activity, students look for words within larger words. Encourage students to make as many words as they can. Challenge students to see who can make the word with the most letters.

Extension idea: Using the reproducible on page 119, provide students with words from a current curricular unit, such as important vocabulary terms from a science lesson. Have each student make lists of words that can be made from selected lesson words.

Sounds Good (pages 51-59)
In this homophone activity, students use homophones (words that sound the same but have different meanings and spellings) to complete sentences. The "Sounds Good" activities begin using one homophone in each sentence and build to using three different homophone words in each sentence.

Extension idea: To extend this activity, have students create their own sentences using homophones. Also, encourage students to share other homophone words with the class when they find them in their readings.

Alphabet Soup (pages 60-67)
In this hidden-words activity, students find a specific word in each line and add a missing letter. When completed, the missing letters will spell out a message.

Extension idea: Students can make their own hidden-words activities using pieces of graph paper. Have each student outline the boxes in the middle of the page. (This is the area where the missing letters will be written.) Since it is sometimes easier to work backwards, have each student lightly write the mystery sentence using a pencil. Then, have her develop a list of related words that contain the letters needed for the mystery sentence. Instruct students to erase their mystery sentences when their lists are complete. Allow students to trade papers to try out each other's homemade "Alphabet Soup" activities.

Word Breakdown (pages 68-75)
In this syllable activity, students take common words and divide them into syllables. Written clues are provided, as well as spaces for each syllable. Using the provided syllable bank, students put the syllables together to provide the correct answers for the clues.

Extension idea: To extend this activity, have students divide other words into syllables, and then write clues for the words. Have students share their activities with classmates or family members.

Letter Sort (pages 76-83)
In this word-scramble activity, students rearrange letters to spell words. Each activity provides a list of scrambled words developed around a theme. When all of the words have been formed, specific letters will be circled. Each student takes the circled letters and arranges them to make words that fit with the themes. The student then uses the letters in the words to make other words.

Extension idea: Students can develop lists of words based on central themes. Then, they can scramble the letters in each word. This is a great activity for students to complete with a younger class. Arrange to have your class work with another, younger class so that your students can teach others how to play with words.

Word Bridges (pages 84-91)
In this hidden-words activity, students search for words that have some letters at the end of one word and the rest of the letters at the beginning of the next word—forming a "bridge" between the two words.

Extension idea: Have students create their own "Word Bridge" sentences using words based on specific themes. Allow students to write their sentences on sentence strips and attach them to a bulletin board for their classmates to solve. Rotate the "Word Bridge" sentences so that each student's sentences are displayed.

Bowling for Letters (pages 92-100)
In this making-words activity, students "bowl" for words. Students are divided into pairs. Each student gets a turn to spell out the longest word by connecting the letters given.

The goal is to get a "strike" by using all 10 letters in one word.

Extension idea: To extend this activity, turn it into a class tournament. Make a transparency of a "Bowling for Letters" activity. Allow students five minutes to create as many words as they can. At the end of the time frame, see which student found the most words and which student found the longest word.

Leap Frog (pages 101-107)
In this activity, students use the provided first compound word or "word buddy" to make additional ones, in order to leap to the end compound word or "word buddy." Students use the words in the Word Bank to create the new words that form connecting "leaps" from the first word to the last word.

Extension idea: Using the reproducible on page 120, have students create their own "Leap Frog" activities. After students have mastered making and playing this activity on paper, make an interactive version using lily pad shapes cut from green felt. Write the challenging words on index cards. These will form the Word Bank for the compound words and "word buddies." Attach hook-and-loop squares to the backs of the cards so that they will adhere to the felt lily pads. Attach the lily pads to a bulletin board. Provide students time to play "Leap Frog" during center time or play as a class.

Look-Alikes (pages 108-117)
In this homograph activity, students find the correct homographs (words that are spelled the same but have different meanings) to complete the sentences.

Extension idea: Challenge students to create a comprehensive class list of common homographs from the "Look-Alikes" activities, as well as other sources. As students bring in additional homographs, list them on poster board. Periodically quiz students on the multiple meanings of these words during regular class routines, such as lining up students for lunch or dismissing students for the day.

An answer key is provided on pages 121–128. Note that some of the answers in the answer key are sample answers since some of the activities have many possibilities.

STEPPING OUT #1

Directions: Starting at the bottom of each ladder, make a new word by adding a letter to each rung. The order of the letters cannot be changed.

1.

beard

be

2.

beast

be

3.

bread

be

9

STEPPING OUT #2

Directions: Starting at the bottom of each ladder, make a new word by adding a letter to each rung. The order of the letters cannot be changed.

1.

began

be

2.

women

me

3.

heard

he

 10

STEPPING OUT #3

Directions: Starting at the bottom of each ladder, make a new word by adding a letter to each rung. The order of the letters cannot be changed.

1.

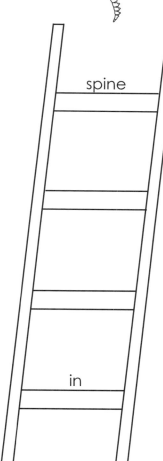

spine

in

2.

twine

in

3.

fined

in

STEPPING OUT #4

Directions: Starting at the bottom of each ladder, make a new word by adding a letter to each rung. The order of the letters cannot be changed.

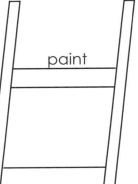

1.

swing

in

2.

paint

it

3.

stone

on

STEPPING OUT #5

Directions: Starting at the bottom of each ladder, make a new word by adding a letter to each rung. The order of the letters cannot be changed.

1.

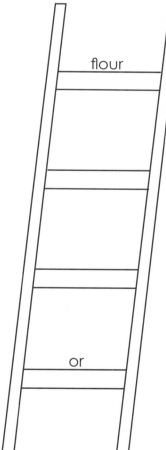

flour

or

2.

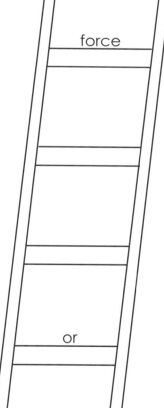

force

or

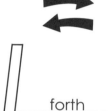

3.

forth

or

STEPPING OUT #6

Directions: Starting at the bottom of each ladder, make a new word by adding a letter to each rung. The order of the letters cannot be changed.

1.

brush

us

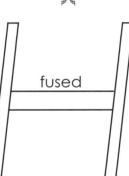

2.

fused

us

3.

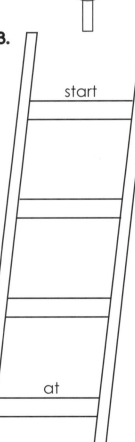

start

at

STEPPING OUT #7

Directions: Starting at the bottom of each ladder, make a new word by adding a letter to each rung. The order of the letters cannot be changed.

1.

hearth

at

2.

charts

as

3.

dreams

am

STEPPING OUT #8

Directions: Starting at the bottom of each ladder, make a new word by adding a letter to each rung. The order of the letters cannot be changed.

1.

chirps

is

2.

splash

as

3.

thinks

in

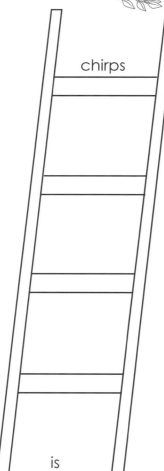
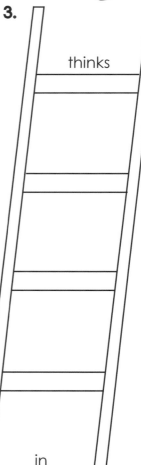

WHAT'S IN THE MIDDLE? #1

Directions: Write the word that fits between each pair of words.

Example: push <u>pin</u> wheel

Word Bank					
ball	car	fly	horse	sand	turtle

1. sea _____ shoe

2. base _____ cap

3. butter _____ ball

4. race _____ pool

5. sea _____ neck

6. quick _____ castle

WHAT'S IN THE MIDDLE? #2

Directions: Write the word that fits between each pair of words.

Example: push <u>pin</u> wheel

Word Bank					
bed	candy	chocolate	milk	paper	watch

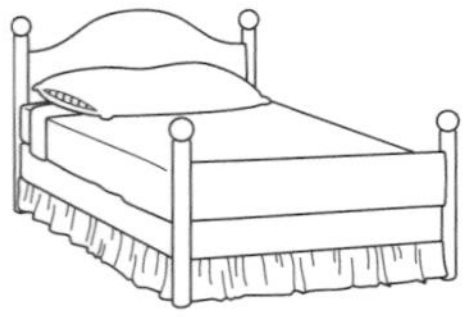

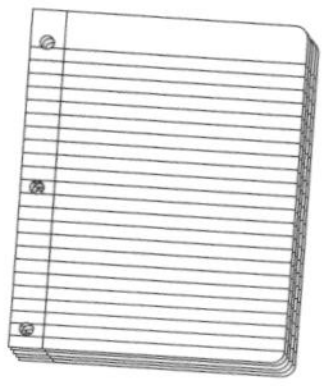

1. wrist _____ tower

2. bunk _____ room

3. chocolate _____ shake

4. hot _____ chip

5. note _____ bag

6. cotton _____ bar

WHAT'S IN THE MIDDLE? #3

Directions: Write the word that fits between each pair of words.

Example: push   <u>pin</u>   wheel

Word Bank					
bike	lion	mouse	party	shoe	wheel

1. mountain _____ ride

2. tennis _____ lace

3. ferris _____ chair

4. mountain _____ tamer

5. tea _____ hat

6. church _____ trap

WHAT'S IN THE MIDDLE? #4

Directions: Write the word that fits between each pair of words.

Example: push <u>pin</u> wheel

Word Bank					
board	box	bus	lunch	room	work

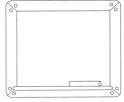

1. chalk _____ walk

2. lunch _____ mate

3. pencil _____ car

4. school _____ stop

5. hot _____ money

6. home _____ out

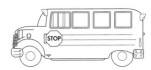

WHAT'S IN THE MIDDLE? #5

Directions: Write the word that fits between each pair of words.

Example: push   <u>pin</u>   wheel

Word Bank					
apple	bean	butter	dog	man	stick

1. corn   _____   house

2. peanut   _____   fly

3. crab   _____   pie

4. carrot   _____   ball

5. handy   _____   hole

6. jelly   _____   bag

WHAT'S IN THE MIDDLE? #6

Directions: Write the word that fits between each pair of words.

Example: push   <u>pin</u>   wheel

Word Bank					
ball	bottle	color	pen	pie	side

1. water _____ neck

2. water _____ blind

3. out _____ line

4. eye _____ room

5. pig _____ pal

6. apple _____ crust

WHAT'S IN THE MIDDLE? #7

Directions: Write the word that fits between each pair of words.

Example: push   <u>pin</u>   wheel

Word Bank					
cup	fish	girl	pan	pin	tree

1. frying   _____   cake

2. tea   _____   cake

3. pine   _____   house

4. gold   _____   stick

5. flower   _____   scout

6. clothes   _____   cushion

WHAT'S IN THE MIDDLE? #8

Directions: Write the word that fits between each pair of words.

Example: push   _pin_   wheel

Word Bank					
bow	box	light	tooth	truck	wash

1. night   _____   bulb

2. tow   _____   stop

3. car   _____   room

4. loose   _____   fairy

5. rain   _____   tie

6. match   _____   car

WHAT'S IN THE MIDDLE? #9

Directions: Write the word that fits between each pair of words.

Example: push   <u>pin</u>   wheel

Word Bank					
dog	frog	hen	pig	sheep	snake

1. hot   _____   collar

2. rattle   _____   skin

3. leap   _____   legs

4. guinea   _____   tail

5. black   _____   herd

6. mother   _____   house

WHAT'S IN THE MIDDLE? #10

Directions: Write the word that fits between each pair of words.

Example: push   <u>pin</u>   wheel

Word Bank					
bird	horse	monster	shell	side	spray

1. sea   _____   bottle

2. sea   _____   house

3. sea   _____   truck

4. sea   _____   race

5. sea   _____   fish

6. sea   _____   walk

HIDDEN WORDS #1

Directions: Use the Word Bank to complete each longer word below.

Word Bank					
EAR	DENT	FAT	HER	LAB	LAG
LENT	MEMO	OR	PEN	RAN	TRICK

1. VETE ___ ___ ___'S DAY

2. ARB ___ ___ DAY

3. F ___ ___ ___ DAY

4. MOT ___ ___ ___'S DAY

5. ___ ___ ___ HER'S DAY

6. VA ___ ___ ___ ___ INE'S DAY

7. SAINT PA ___ ___ ___ ___ ___'S DAY

8. PRESI ___ ___ ___ ___S' DAY

9. ___ ___ ___ TH DAY

10. INDE ___ ___ ___ DENCE DAY

11. ___ ___ ___ ___ RIAL DAY

12. ___ ___ ___ OR DAY

HIDDEN WORDS #2

Directions: Use the Word Bank to complete each longer word below.

Word Bank					
ACE	AGE	ANT	ATE	BE	HI
IF	JAM	OAT	ON	SO	TOW

1. UN ___ ___ ORM

2. SK ___ ___ ___ S

3. ___ ___ ___ EL

4. NECKL ___ ___ ___

5. BAND ___ ___ ___

6. S ___ ___ RT

7. PA ___ ___ ___ AS

8. ___ ___ LT

9. APR ___ ___

10. P ___ ___ ___ S

11. ___ ___ CKS

12. C ___ ___ ___

HIDDEN WORDS #3

Directions: Use the Word Bank to complete each longer word below.

Word Bank					
ACE	CUB	FRO	HOW	ICE	INK
INK	NO	REAM	SHE	SO	TEA

1. JU ___ ___ ___

2. DR ___ ___ ___

3. ICE C ___ ___ ___ ___

4. ___ ___ ___ RBET

5. ___ ___ DA

6. ICE ___ ___ ___ E

7. S ___ ___ ___ M

8. ___ ___ ___ ST

9. S ___ ___ ___ ER

10. R ___ ___ ___

11. SPR ___ ___ ___ LE

12. S ___ ___ W

29

HIDDEN WORDS #4

Directions: Use the Word Bank to complete each longer word below.

Word Bank					
ALL	ART	BAN	CHAR	DIM	DOLL
END	HANG	HE	IN	ONE	PEN

1. C ___ ___ ___ ___ E

2. C ___ ___ CK

3. ___ ___ ___ ___ AR

4. ___ ___ ___ K

5. ___ ___ ___ E

6. ___ ___ ___ NY

7. ___ ___ ___ ___ GE

8. SP ___ ___ ___

9. QU ___ ___ ___ ER

10. CO ___ ___

11. M ___ ___ ___ Y

12. W ___ ___ ___ ET

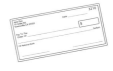

HIDDEN WORDS #5

Directions: Use the Word Bank to complete each longer word below.

Word Bank					
AN	ATE	BOW	ILL	IN	IT
IT	ITCH	KEY	ON	PEN	TO

1. TUR ___ ___ ___

2. S ___ ___ MACH

3. T ___ ___ K

4. P ___ ___ ___ ___ ER

5. P ___ ___ ___ OW

6. ___ ___ ___ L

7. S ___ ___ K

8. SU ___ ___ CASE

9. CAV ___ ___ Y

10. O ___ ___ ___ ING

11. C ___ ___ TAINER

12. PL ___ ___ ___

HIDDEN WORDS #6

Directions: Use the Word Bank to complete each longer word below.

Word Bank					
AM	DO	GO	IS	LET	LOB
ON	OR	ROOST	SHE	TEN	USE

1. M __O__ __T__ KEY

2. H __am__ STER

3. MO __use__

4. H __OR__ SE

5. ___ ___ AT

6. ___ ___ ___ EP

7. __DO__ G

8. PIG ___ ___ ___

9. __Roost__ ER

10. KIT __Ien__

11. __Lob__ STER

12. F __i__ __s__ H

32

HIDDEN WORDS #7

Directions: Use the Word Bank to complete each longer word below.

Word Bank					
ACT	CAME	DIRE	HEAR	HEAT	ICE
MAN	ON	RIP	TAG	TICK	VIE

1. __ __ __ OR

2. __ __ __ __ RA

3. __ __ __ __ CTOR

4. SC __ __ __ T

5. S __ __ __ E

6. RE __ __ __ __ SAL

7. ACTI __ __

8. PERFOR __ __ __ CE

9. RE __ __ __ W

10. T __ __ __ __ ER

11. BOX OFF __ __ __

12. __ __ __ __ ETS

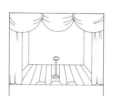

BOX OFFICE

HIDDEN WORDS #8

Directions: Use the Word Bank to complete each longer word below.

Word Bank					
ARCH	DEN	DENT	EACH	EDIT	LAW
LOT	OR	PAL	PORT	RAM	RAN

1. T ___ ___ ___ ___ ER

2. ___ ___ ___ TIST

3. DOCT ___ ___

4. PRINCI ___ ___ ___

5. ___ ___ ___ YER

6. PRESI ___ ___ ___ ___

7. RE ___ ___ ___ ___ ER

8. ___ ___ ___ ___ OR

9. PA ___ ___ ___ EDIC

10. ___ ___ ___ GER

11. ___ ___ ___ ___ ITECT

12. PI ___ ___ ___

34

WHAT'S IN COMMON? #1

Directions: Sort the words into the various categories. Each word can only be used in one blank. Be careful of words that could be placed in more than one category.

Word Bank				
basketball	beach	butterfly	cleats	cotton
cowboy	drag	driving	fishing	gardening
hair	heels	horse	human	slippers
	soccer	top	visor	

gloves			
balls			
shoes			
race			
nets			
hats			

WHAT'S IN COMMON? #2

Directions: Sort the words into the various categories. Each word can only be used in one blank. Be careful of words that could be placed in more than one category.

Word Bank				
albatross	chicken	claws	down	duck
emu	flamingo	ostrich	peacock	pelican
penguin	plume	seagull	talon	toucan
	turkey	waterproof	webbed	

seabirds			
poultry			
flightless birds			
colorful birds			
feather characteristics			
feet characteristics			

WHAT'S IN COMMON? #3

Directions: Sort the words into the various categories. Each word can only be used in one blank. Be careful of words that could be placed in more than one category.

Word Bank			
ball	castle	cherry	flake
foot	hut	man	meter
mile	princess	queen	ruler
soil	stop sign	strawberry	spade
tepee	vegetable		

homes			
red			
garden			
royalty			
measure			
snow			

WHAT'S IN COMMON? #4

Directions: Sort the words into the various categories. Each word can only be used in one blank. Be careful of words that could be placed in more than one category.

Word Bank				
car	classmates	cornea	duo	goggles
iris	learners	pair	peers	pupil
snapdragon	spectacles	sun	swimming	tulip
	twins	wading	zinnia	

eye				
students		classmates		
flowers				
glasses				
pools				
twos	222	pair	twins	

WHAT'S IN COMMON? #5

Directions: Sort the words into the various categories. Each word can only be used in one blank. Be careful of words that could be placed in more than one category.

Word Bank				
bars	board	cards	chain	crossword
garbanzo	jeans	jigsaw	kidney	lima
mine	moon	pinkie	sky	telephone
	toss	trivia	word search	

gold			
ring			
blue			
games			
puzzles			
beans			

WHAT'S IN COMMON? #6

Directions: Sort the words into the various categories. Each word can only be used in one blank. Be careful of words that could be placed in more than one category.

Word Bank				
apple	chocolate	cracked	Danish	garlic
grape	hot	oatmeal	orange	puff
rice	rye	scrambled	shake	shell
	strudel	white	whole	

egg			
pastry			
milk			
juice			
bread			
cereal			

WHAT'S IN COMMON? #7

Directions: Sort the words into the various categories. Each word can only be used in one blank. Be careful of words that could be placed in more than one category.

Word Bank				
beaver	book	chipmunk	construction	grocery
invitation	keyboard	newspaper	notebook	magazine
math	monitor	mouse	reading	science
	spelling	squirrel	wrapping	

paper				
computer				
subject				
lists				
rodents				
things to read				

WHAT'S IN COMMON? #8

Directions: Sort the words into the various categories. Each word can only be used in one blank. Be careful of words that could be placed in more than one category.

Word Bank				
address	bottles	cards	coins	confetti
door	folders	gifts	greeting	hands
helmet	hood	motor	name	stamps
	wig	window	wishes	

things that hold			
parts of a letter			
collectibles			
birthday items			
head coverings			
car parts			

IN OTHER WORDS #1

Directions: Make as many words as you can using the letters from both words below.

Example: bedroom
Words that can be made: be, bed, broom, Ed, doom, room

elephant

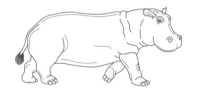

hippopotamus

1. _____	1. _____
2. _____	2. _____
3. _____	3. _____
4. _____	4. _____
5. _____	5. _____
6. _____	6. _____
7. _____	7. _____
8. _____	8. _____
9. _____	9. _____
10. _____	10. _____
11. _____	11. _____
12. _____	12. _____

IN OTHER WORDS #2

Directions: Make as many words as you can using the letters from both words below.

Example: bedroom
Words that can be made: be, bed, broom, Ed, doom, room

hamburger

pancakes

1. _____
2. _____
3. _____
4. _____
5. _____
6. _____
7. _____
8. _____
9. _____
10. _____
11. _____
12. _____

1. _____
2. _____
3. _____
4. _____
5. _____
6. _____
7. _____
8. _____
9. _____
10. _____
11. _____
12. _____

IN OTHER WORDS #3

Directions: Make as many words as you can using the letters from both words below.

Example: bedroom
Words that can be made: be, bed, broom, Ed, doom, room

computers   reading

1. _____   1. _____
2. _____   2. _____
3. _____   3. _____
4. _____   4. _____
5. _____   5. _____
6. _____   6. _____
7. _____   7. _____
8. _____   8. _____
9. _____   9. _____
10. _____   10. _____
11. _____   11. _____
12. _____   12. _____

IN OTHER WORDS #4

Directions: Make as many words as you can using the letters from both words below.

Example: bedroom
Words that can be made: be, bed, broom, Ed, doom, room

decorate

presents

1. _____
2. _____
3. _____
4. _____
5. _____
6. _____
7. _____
8. _____
9. _____
10. _____
11. _____
12. _____

1. _____
2. _____
3. _____
4. _____
5. _____
6. _____
7. _____
8. _____
9. _____
10. _____
11. _____
12. _____

IN OTHER WORDS #5

Directions: Make as many words as you can using the letters from both words below.

Example: bedroom
Words that can be made: be, bed, broom, Ed, doom, room

accordion

xylophone

1. _____	1. _____
2. _____	2. _____
3. _____	3. _____
4. _____	4. _____
5. _____	5. _____
6. _____	6. _____
7. _____	7. _____
8. _____	8. _____
9. _____	9. _____
10. _____	10. _____
11. _____	11. _____
12. _____	12. _____

47

IN OTHER WORDS #6

Directions: Make as many words as you can using the letters from both words below.

Example: bedroom
Words that can be made: be, bed, broom, Ed, doom, room

Lincoln

Washington

1. _____	1. _____
2. _____	2. _____
3. _____	3. _____
4. _____	4. _____
5. _____	5. _____
6. _____	6. _____
7. _____	7. _____
8. _____	8. _____
9. _____	9. _____
10. _____	10. _____
11. _____	11. _____
12. _____	12. _____

IN OTHER WORDS #7

Directions: Make as many words as you can using the letters from both words below.

Example: bedroom
Words that can be made: be, bed, broom, Ed, doom, room

Australia

North America

Australia	North America
1. _____	1. _____
2. _____	2. _____
3. _____	3. _____
4. _____	4. _____
5. _____	5. _____
6. _____	6. _____
7. _____	7. _____
8. _____	8. _____
9. _____	9. _____
10. _____	10. _____
11. _____	11. _____
12. _____	12. _____

IN OTHER WORDS #8

Directions: Make as many words as you can using the letters from both words below.

Example: bedroom
Words that can be made: be, bed, broom, Ed, doom, room

Mount Rushmore

Mount Kilimanjaro

1. _____
2. _____
3. _____
4. _____
5. _____
6. _____
7. _____
8. _____
9. _____
10. _____
11. _____
12. _____

1. _____
2. _____
3. _____
4. _____
5. _____
6. _____
7. _____
8. _____
9. _____
10. _____
11. _____
12. _____

SOUNDS GOOD #1

Homophones are sets of words that sound the same but have different meanings and spellings. For example:

arc—part of a circle   ark—a boat

Directions: Complete each pair of sentences with the correct homophones.

base
bass

1. My sister plays the _____ clarinet.

2. The baseball player stole third _____.

lay
lei

3. A _____ is a necklace made of flowers.

4. Did you _____ the baby in her crib?

loot
lute

5. The thief tried to sell the _____.

6. She plays the _____ beautifully.

stake
steak

7. Tie the plant to the _____.

8. How do you want the _____ cooked?

vary
very

9. The answers will _____.

10. It was a _____ good book.

SOUNDS GOOD #2

Homophones are sets of words that sound the same but have different meanings and spellings. For example:

beach—a shore

beech—a tree

Directions: Complete each pair of sentences with the correct homophones.

bazaar
bizarre

1. Many things can be bought at the _____.
2. The man's behavior was _____.

aisle
isle

3. Each summer, many people visit the _____.
4. Who will walk her down the _____?

billed
build

5. Who can _____ a skyscraper?
6. The duck-_____ platypus is odd looking.

seam
seem

7. Does her hair _____ the same?
8. He ripped the _____ on his pants.

find
fined

9. Help me _____ my glasses.
10. The driver was _____ for speeding.

SOUNDS GOOD #3

Homophones are sets of words that sound the same but have different meanings and spellings. For example:

 sea—an ocean   see—to view

Directions: Complete each pair of sentences with the correct homophones.

cells
sells

1. The honeycomb contains many _____.
2. Erik _____ trading cards.

brake
break

3. Please do not _____ the dishes.
4. The car has a hand _____.

sight
site

5. The construction _____ is around the corner.
6. The dancing dog was quite a _____.

flair
flare

7. She has a _____ for decorating.
8. Be careful when lighting the _____.

fair
fare

9. How much is the bus _____?
10. When will the _____ come to town?

SOUNDS GOOD #4

Homophones are sets of words that sound the same but have different meanings and spellings. For example:

 wail—to cry   whale—a large sea animal

Directions: Complete each pair of sentences with the correct homophones.

toad	towed	
sheer	shear	

1. The _____ sat on the _____ surface.
2. He had to _____ the sheep's wool before it was _____ to the fair.

cereal	serial
chews	choose

3. Lola _____ the _____ loudly.
4. Which _____ novels did you _____?

banned	band
guessed	guest

5. The last _____ to leave the party was _____ from talking so much.
6. I _____ which _____ would perform.

mail	male
allowed	aloud

7. The _____ gorilla was _____ to eat bananas.
8. The singer's fan _____ was read _____.

foul	fowl
peer	pier

9. The _____ is sitting on the _____.
10. The player was happy to see his _____ make the _____ shot.

Play Word Play Word Play Word Play Word

SOUNDS GOOD #5

Homophones are sets of words that sound the same but have different meanings and spellings. For example:

tied— formed into a knot   tide—an ocean's movement

Directions: Complete each pair of sentences with the correct homophones.

| gate | gait |
| hear | here |

1. I can _____ the horse's steady _____.
2. _____ is the _____ to the backyard.

| coop | coupe |
| for | four |

3. Mom bought a _____ with _____ wheels.
4. The _____ is _____ the chickens.

| vain | vane |
| tern | turn |

5. The _____ will _____ in the wind.
6. The arctic _____ is considered a _____ bird.

| guest | guessed |
| cheap | cheep |

7. The dinner _____ can _____ like a bird.
8. She _____ the cost would be _____.

| base | bass |
| beat | beet |

9. The _____ drum sets a strong _____.
10. A _____ is the _____ ingredient in borscht.

SOUNDS GOOD #6

Homophones are sets of words that sound the same but have different meanings and spellings. For example:

 read—to recognize words   reed—an instrument

Directions: Complete each pair of sentences with the correct homophones.

| heard | herd |
| jam | jamb |

1. The cattle _____ was in a _____ near the gate.

2. We _____ a squeal when he caught his finger in the door _____.

| colonel | kernel |
| flew | flu |

3. The _____ has the _____.

4. The popcorn _____ _____ by her head.

| ball | bawl |
| throne | thrown |

5. The _____ _____ landed in the catcher's mitt.

6. The sad queen will _____ from her _____.

| plain | plane |
| stair | stare |

7. I saw him _____ at the _____ piece of paper.

8. The toy _____ is on the top _____.

| band | banned |
| blew | blue |

9. The _____ _____ away the crowd!

10. _____ hair has been _____ at her school.

SOUNDS GOOD #7

Homophones are sets of words that sound the same but have different meanings and spellings. For example:

 hangar—aircraft storage   hanger—an object to hold clothes

Directions: Complete each pair of sentences with the correct homophones.

ant   aunt
Bea   bee
two   to

1. My _____ _____ has _____ children.
2. I gave water _____ the _____ and the _____.

eye   I
ate   eight
hole   whole

3. _____ can't believe I _____ the _____ thing!
4. My left _____ saw the _____-foot-deep _____.

carat   carrot
doe   dough
ewe   you

5. _____ should take off the two-_____ diamond ring before making the _____.
6. The _____ and the _____ ate the _____.

knight night
sail   sale
sea   see

7. The _____ set _____ on the high _____.
8. I _____ that the _____ begins tomorrow _____ at nine o' clock.

knot   not
one   won
right   write

9. After they _____ the game, she untied the _____ in her _____ shoelace.
10. Do _____ _____ only _____ letter to the entire family!

NAME_____   DATE_____

SOUNDS GOOD #8

Homophones are sets of words that sound the same but have different meanings and spellings. For example:

    shear—to cut   sheer—transparent

Directions: Complete each pair of sentences with the correct homophones.

flour   flower
sew   so
son   sun

1. Her _____ will _____ the _____ on the shirt.

2. The boy was _____ tired after grinding the _____ in the _____.

pail   pale
read   red
close   clothes

3. _____ the _____ door by the _____.

4. She _____ the tags on the _____ yellow _____.

hour   our
road   rode
rose   rows

5. The _____ went by _____ _____bushes.

6. In one _____, we _____ to the _____ of corn.

muscle   mussel
toe   tow
weak   week

7. Her middle _____ has a pretty _____ _____.

8. Last _____, the _____ was in _____ in the swirling waves.

naval   navel
peace   piece
role   roll

9. The _____ officer's _____ is to keep the _____.

10. _____ a _____ of the _____ orange in the honey.

SOUNDS GOOD #9

Homophones are sets of words that sound the same but have different meanings and spellings. For example:

toad—a common amphibian   towed—pulled

Directions: Complete each pair of sentences with the correct homophones.

bell	belle
cent	sent
tea	tee

1. The prince _____ a cup of _____ to the _____ of the ball.

2. He struck the cheap, five-_____ _____ harder than a golfer hits a ball off a _____.

bare	bear
chili	chilly
hair	hare

3. The _____ with _____ could smell the _____.

4. The _____ was _____ since it was _____.

in	inn
main	Maine
pair	pear

5. I ate an entire _____ pie when I stayed at the _____ in _____.

6. The _____ live _____ the _____ house.

ad	add
ewe	you
pain	pane

7. The _____ shows a sheared _____ without _____.

8. _____ need to _____ a _____ to the window.

minor	miner
no	know
to	two

9. The gem _____ went _____ Virginia and did not _____ what she would find.

10. The _____ character had _____ more than _____ lines in the play.

ALPHABET SOUP #1

Directions: Add a letter from the letter bank to each set of letters to create a word. Circle the complete word. The missing letters spell out a message.

A	A	A	D	I	N	O	O	P	R	R	T

1. K S A B A L L   O N R I Q R A

2. Q Z Z P A V A   A B Z D J H R

3. A Y O S U B W   Y G K I T J J

4. H I J X Y B T   U C K F L W L

5. X F S T A T I   N W A G O N B

6. D P K W C B O   T Q S E U I M

7. W Y B G G O N   O L A X H H P

8. E V C A V M O   O R C Y C L E

9. M D U C N L T   A I N O S F S

10. D N V W A L K   N G T G N T W

11. U O M G A I R   L A N E F E M

ALPHABET SOUP #2

Directions: Add a letter from the letter bank to each set of letters to create a word.
Circle the complete word. The missing letters spell out a message.

A	E	F	F	I	S	S	T	T	T	Y

1. U Z H A A O Q ☐ L O R I D A A

2. B K P V R L B ☐ D A H O B P I

3. I M H C A L I ☐ O R N I A S D

4. T J N C Q N U ☐ A H J Y O D V

5. O F U D C L W ☐ O M I N G I M

6. U E W L O U I ☐ I A N A H R E

7. W A S H I N G ☐ O N Z R K Y E

8. L F P K A N S ☐ S A X G X K X

9. W L D S Q C D ☐ E X A S W S H

10. Y T B F V G G ☐ O R G I A M F

11. N J A R K A N ☐ A S E I A T G

ALPHABET SOUP #3

Directions: Add a letter from the letter bank to each set of letters to create a word. Circle the complete word. The missing letters spell out a message.

A	A	A	A	D	E	E	F	I	T	V	Y

1.   A C U C U M B ☐ R P A P U X G

2.   Q B W F B A N ☐ N A Y O R V B

3.   H Y N T O M A ☐ O T E Q V O Z

4.   U A S W I D C ☐ I G N S M T D

5.   R Z C E U S P ☐ N A C H T B M

6.   E L C W J R A ☐ O C A D O S V

7.   D S Q A P P L ☐ P L K P U E M

8.   K T F F F Q C ☐ R R O T N W K

9.   G V G X J M L ☐ A T E L R P B

10.   O G Y H M G R ☐ P E I J K Y W

11.   H Z C H E R R ☐ A X J H N I I

ALPHABET SOUP #4

Directions: Add a letter from the letter bank to each set of letters to create a word. Circle the complete word. The missing letters spell out a message.

A	C	E	H	N	O	O	P	P	P	R	S	S	T

#				
1.	T M O T I O N	[ ]	I C T U R E U
2.	H J G C B V C	[ ]	N D Y W B W J
3.	C U R T A I N	[ ]	T A R E A T S
4.	R A F S E A T	[ ]	I A Q C Y K F
5.	W Z D A R Q A	[ ]	I C K E T P Z
6.	P Y E L A U G	[ ]	D O Y T S C O
7.	C I E X C I T	[ ]	M E N T D N D
8.	A N H A G R Y	[ ]	R O J E C T K
9.	O U P H A N M	[ ]	V I E N A C E
10.	H J P E L E R	[ ]	L O T T I H C
11.	I H P S E N S	[ ]	R E E N G J R
12.	F V Q R K S L	[ ]	B B Y I N E E
13.	P D C A C T O	[ ]	S L L A L D O
14.	B L A C T I O	[ ]	K I R G H M A

ALPHABET SOUP #5

Directions: Add a letter from the letter bank to each set of letters to create a word. Circle the complete word. The missing letters spell out a message.

A E H I I O O S S T T T U V Z

1.	R A T Q W O L		E S Y P I Z B
2.	M X T G E A G		R A F F E S L
3.	R Y H P O B N		N A K E S S U
4.	P K H M K L H		P P O S A J Q
5.	O S P A R R O		S M N R S B B
6.	L Y E D J A G		A R S J I I R
7.	G X W A L R U		E S J A J D A
8.	R I K N D T P		N D A S H E M
9.	O G X C V C J		I G E R S H D
10.	Z Q K R T U R		L E S B I U B
11.	F G U E L E P		A N T S W S M
12.	D Z Q P C A M		L S P F N V H
13.	W G K V O E W		E B R A S L V
14.	F W N E B E X		W L S U C D T
15.	Y K A N G A R		O S M D L O D

ALPHABET SOUP #6

Directions: Add a letter from the letter bank to each set of letters to create a word. Circle the complete word. The missing letters spell out a message.

| C | E | E | E | E | G | H | M | M | N | O | O | R | R | T | Y |

1.	A E O Q E R S		I T C H E S B
2.	D H Q V D S P		O S P I T A L
3.	P O W C W U B		D X N R Q A F
4.	Y S F F L O W		R S S D O I N
5.	Z M C T H E R		O M E T E R Z
6.	U M B K V O M		D I C I N E L
7.	N S K T Y P A		A M E D I C R
8.	C Y B A N D A		E S L Y T P T
9.	D K X N U R S		R E J M D E F
10.	L A M B U L A		C E R Q Z P B
11.	A B U D D J T		A S T K J X Z
12.	N I I U X R A		K O U W L N E
13.	A J H T J S U		G E R Y V C U
14.	I A F F M M D		C T O R L H G
15.	W S H G V H G		W N S B G S G
16.	H I N S T R U		E N T S I V W

ALPHABET SOUP #7

Directions: Add a letter from the letter bank to each set of letters to create a word. Circle the complete word. The missing letters spell out a message.

A	A	C	E	E	F	I	L	L	M	O	R	R	S	T	W

1. A I X S T R A ☐ B E R R Y F P

2. T F H C O F F ☐ E B A R P N B

3. Y C B A N A N ☐ P A C O G M X

4. L R O V A N I ☐ L A D G L I D

5. S G M S W I R ☐ O F E I E B V

6. A B U T T E R ☐ C O T C H H Z

7. G S G U C H O ☐ O L A T E M Q

8. J L R O C K Y ☐ O A D H I Y B

9. I T H R G Q L ☐ M O N P D M J

10. J X K F L C C ☐ N D I E S J R

11. I S K E Y L I ☐ E M E T A U B

12. L A V K W A F ☐ L E C O N E Z

13. C O O K I E D ☐ U G H C H A I

14. A U F U D G E ☐ O Y A L Y X O

15. O Y M E C S T ☐ C E C R E A M

16. P Q R S M I N ☐ P Q M O R I W

ALPHABET SOUP #8

Directions: Add a letter from the letter bank to each set of letters to create a word. Circle the complete word. The missing letters spell out a message.

A A E E E G H L L M P S S T T Y

1.	D S C R A S O	☐	I T A I R E E
2.	A Y J D N C H	☐	S S I O C J Y
3.	Q P E R T I C	☐	A C T O E X A
4.	N X Z G O F I	☐	H M O N K M E
5.	V O W M O N O	☐	O I N T S B P
6.	F L C A N D P	☐	A Y E R S A N
7.	A F L L O M M	☐	R B L E S V O
8.	S T R A T E G	☐	A H W Z E E W
9.	C H O P S C O	☐	C H B T K H L
10.	Q V E X U D C	☐	E C K E R S G
11.	N B L I R U L	☐	S U I P K Q P
12.	J M G D B O C	☐	O A L T T D G
13.	T J B A C K G	☐	M M O N N W Q
14.	I H K H M J U	☐	O V E S U J C
15.	U S E A M U S	☐	M E N T Q N R
16.	J G I S L G R	☐	P O R T H F I

WORD BREAKDOWN #1

Directions: Use the syllable bank to answer each clue about a United States president. Write the syllables on the lines. Each syllable is used once.

CAR	CLIN	COLN	GAN	HOO	ING
LIN	NIX	ON	REA	ROO	SE
TER	TON	TON	VELT	VER	WASH

1. First president   _ _ _ _ _ + _ _ _ _ + _ _ _

2. Elected in 1932   _ _ _ + _ _ _ + _ _ _ _ _

3. 16th president   _ _ _ _ + _ _ _ _ _

4. Born August 10, 1874   _ _ _ + _ _ _ _

5. Winner of the Nobel Peace Prize   _ _ _ + _ _ _ _

6. Former actor   _ _ _ _ + _ _ _ _

7. Born in Hope, Arkansas   _ _ _ _ _ + _ _ _ _

8. Preceded Gerald Ford   _ _ _ + _ _ _

WORD BREAKDOWN #2

Directions: Use the syllable bank to answer each clue. Write the syllables on the lines. Each syllable is used once.

A	CHES	ENCE	HIS	ING	ING	ING
ME	MU	OR	READ	RITH	SCI	SIC
SPELL	TIC	TOR	TRA	WRIT	Y	

1. Can be done in a group or silently __ __ __ __ + __ __ __

2. Need to use a pen or pencil __ __ __ __ + __ __ __

3. Multiply, divide, add, or subtract. __ + __ __ __ __ __ + __ __ + __ __ __

4. Events that happened in the past __ __ __ + __ __ __ __ + __

5. Look it up! __ __ __ __ __ + __ __ __

6. Doing experiments __ __ __ + __ __ __ __

7. Making music with instruments __ __ + __ __ __ __ __ + __ __ __

8. Instruments playing and voices singing __ __ + __ __ __

WORD BREAKDOWN #3

Directions: Use the syllable bank to answer each clue. Write the syllables on the lines. Each syllable is used once.

BAD	BALL	BALL	BAS	CER	CRO	EY
GYM	HOCK	KET	LEY	MIN	NAS	NIS
QUET	SOC	TEN	TICS	TON	VOL	

1. Often played on the beach   _ _ _ + _ _ _ + _ _ _ _

2. Many call it football instead.   _ _ _ + _ _ _

3. Played with a puck and sticks   _ _ _ _ _ + _ _

4. Involves a lot of flexibility and strength   _ _ _ + _ _ _ _ + _ _ _ _ _

5. Played on a lawn with wickets and mallets   _ _ _ + _ _ _ _ _

6. Uses long, skinny rackets and a tall net   _ _ _ + _ _ _ _ + _ _ _ _

7. Played with a hoop and a ball   _ _ _ + _ _ _ _ + _ _ _ _

8. Played on clay or grass courts   _ _ _ + _ _ _ _

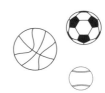

WORD BREAKDOWN #4

Directions: Use the syllable bank to answer each clue. Write the syllables on the lines. Each syllable is used once.

A	A	A	AL	BAM	CAL	COL	CON	DO
FORN	HA	I	I	IA	KA	LAND	LAS	MAR
NEW	O	RA	SIN	WAI	WIS	Y	YORK	

1. Montgomery   __ __ + __ + __ __ __ + __

2. Sacramento   __ __ __ + __ + __ __ __ + __ __ __

3. Honolulu   __ __ + __ __ __ + __

4. Juneau   __ + __ __ __ + __ __

5. Denver   __ __ __ + __ + __ __ + __ __

6. Albany   __ __ __ + __ __ __ __

7. Annapolis   __ __ __ + __ + __ __ __ __

8. Madison   __ __ __ + __ __ __ + __ __ __ __

WORD BREAKDOWN #5

Directions: Use the syllable bank to answer each clue. Write the syllables on the lines. Each syllable is used once.

A	A	AL	BOX	CE	DI	DI	I
LET	MAG	MES	NEWS	PA	PE	PER	RE
REC	REC	RY	SAGE	TER	TIONS	ZINE	

1. Tells what's going on each day   __ __ __ __ + __ __ + __ __ __

2. Read for fun or for information   __ __ __ + __ + __ __ __ __ __

3. A place to write secrets   __ __ + __ + __ __

4. Found on a breakfast table   __ __ + __ __ + __ __ + __ __ __

5. Placed in a mailbox   __ __ __ + __ __ __

6. Explains how to do something   __ __ + __ __ __ + __ __ __ __ __

7. Followed when cooking   __ __ __ + __ + __ __

8. Found in a bottle or beside the phone   __ __ __ + __ __ __ __

WORD BREAKDOWN #6

Directions: Use the syllable bank to answer each clue. Write the syllables on the lines. Each syllable is used once.

A	CAM	CHA	E	EL	EL	ER	GA	HIP
KAN	LEON	LI	ME	MUS	NOC	O	ON	OS
PHANT	PO	POT	RANG	RHI	ROO	TAN	U	

1. Has a long trunk

   _ _ + _ + _ _ _ _ _

2. A really big cat

   _ _ + _ _

3. Has one or two horns

   _ _ _ + _ _ _ + _ _ + _ _

4. A river mammal

   _ _ _ + _ _ + _ _ _ + _ + _ _ _

5. A shaggy-coated ape

   _ + _ _ _ _ + _ + _ _ _

6. A jumping animal from Australia

   _ _ _ + _ _ + _ _ _

7. Can change its colors

   _ _ _ + _ _ + _ _ _ _

8. Able to store water

   _ _ _ + _ _

WORD BREAKDOWN #7

Directions: Use the syllable bank to answer each clue. Write the syllables on the lines. Each syllable is used once.

AN	BRAR	CAR	CHAN	CI	DENT	ER	ER	GA
I	I	I	IC	LI	ME	NAV	PAL	PEN
PHO	PRES	PRIN	RAPH	TEACH	TER	TOG	TOR	

1. Helps students learn   __ __ __ __ __ + __ __

2. Head of a school   __ __ __ __ + __ __ + __ __ __

3. Takes pictures   __ __ __ + __ __ __ + __ __ __ __ + __ __

4. Works on cars   __ __ + __ __ __ __ + __ __

5. Builds things with wood   __ __ __ + __ __ __ __ + __ __ __

6. Sets the course on a ship or plane   __ __ __ + __ + __ __ + __ __ __

7. Works around a lot of books   __ __ + __ __ __ __ + __ + __ __

8. Leader of the United States   __ __ __ __ + __ + __ __ __ __

WORD BREAKDOWN #8

Directions: Use the syllable bank to answer each clue. Write the syllables on the lines. Each syllable is used once.

BAS	BAS	BUCK	CON	EN	ER	ER
ET	ETS	FOLD	KET	LOPE	NET	ON
POCK	SI	TAIN	VE	WAG		

1. Papers are neatly placed in this.   _ _ _ _ + _ _

2. Gathered eggs can go in this.   _ _ _ + _ _ _

3. Leftovers can go in this.   _ _ _ + _ _ _ _ + _ _

4. A baby might sleep in this.   _ _ _ + _ _ + _ _ _

5. This has four wheels and is often red.   _ _ _ + _ _

6. A letter is mailed in one of these.   _ _ + _ _ + _ _ _ _

7. These are usually found on the backs of jeans.   _ _ _ _ + _ _ _

8. This can hold sand or water.   _ _ _ _ + _ _

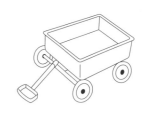

LETTER SORT #1

Directions: Rearrange each set of letters to name a subject or activity. Write the letters on the lines. Then, follow the directions below.

1. EGHILNS   __ __ __ __ __ __ __

2. EGILLNPS   __ __ __ __ __ __ __ __

3. GIINRTW   __ __ __ ◯ __ __ __

4. AHMT   __ ◯ __ __

5. ADEGINR   __ __ __ __ ◯ __ __

6. CCEEINS   __ __ __ __ __ ◯ __

7. CIMSU   ◯ __ __ __ __

8. ABDN   __ __ ◯ __

9. ACEHORRST   __ __ __ __ ◯ __ __ __ __

10. ABILRRY   __ __ __ __ __ __ __

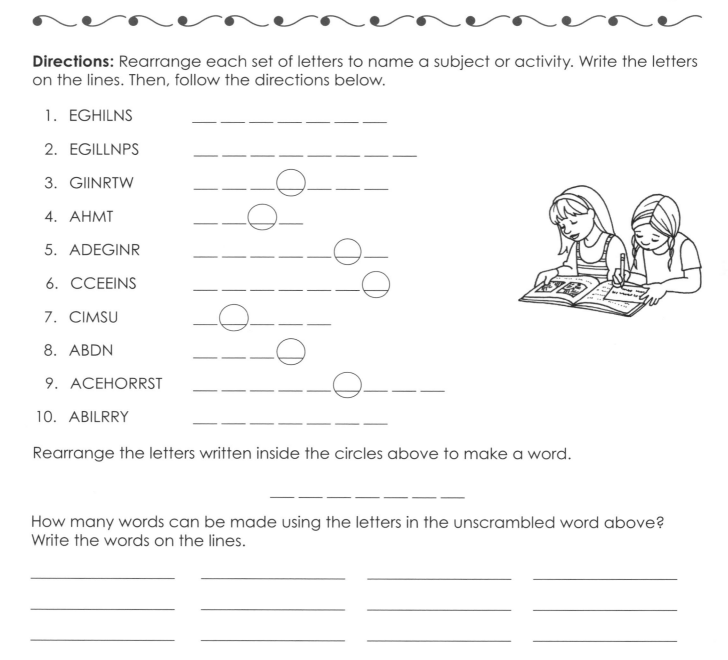

Rearrange the letters written inside the circles above to make a word.

__ __ __ __ __ __ __ __

How many words can be made using the letters in the unscrambled word above? Write the words on the lines.

_____ _____ _____ _____

_____ _____ _____ _____

_____ _____ _____ _____

LETTER SORT #2

Directions: Rearrange each set of letters to name a green object. Write the letters on the lines. Then, follow the directions below.

1. BCCILOOR   __ __◯__ __ __ __ __

2. AEELSV   __ __ __ __◯__

3. FGORS   ◯__ __ __ __

4. AGRSS   __◯__ __ __

5. EILMS   __ __ __ __ __

6. ADILRSZ   __ __ __ __ __ __ __

7. AAGILLORST   __ __ __ __ __◯__ __ __

8. CELORV   __ __ __ __ __ __

9. CEELRY   __ __ __◯__ __

10. ADEELMRS   __ __ __ __ __ __◯__

Rearrange the letters written inside the circles above to make a word.

__ __ __ __ __ __ __

How many words can be made using the letters in the unscrambled word above? Write the words on the lines.

_____   _____   _____   _____

_____   _____   _____   _____

_____   _____   _____   _____

LETTER SORT #3

Directions: Rearrange each set of letters to name a nationality. Write the letters on the lines. Then, follow the directions below.

1. CEFHNR   __ __◯__ __ __

2. AEGMNR   __◯__ __ __ __

3. EGHILNS __ __ __ __ __ __

4. AHINPSS __◯__ __ __ __

5. AINRSSU __ __ __ __ __ __

6. CEEHINS __ __ __ __ __ __

7. AAEEJNPS __ __◯__ __ __ __

8. AEKNOR   __◯__ __ __ __

9. AHIILSW __ __ __ __ __◯__

10. CDHTU   __ __ __ __ __

Rearrange the letters written inside the circles above to make a word.

__ __ __ __ __ __ __

How many words can be made using the letters in the unscrambled word above? Write the words on the lines.

_____ _____ _____ _____

_____ _____ _____ _____

_____ _____ _____ _____

LETTER SORT #4

Directions: Rearrange each set of letters to name a musical instrument. Write the letters on the lines. Then, follow the directions below.

1. IILNOV   __ __ (__) __ __ __

2. AINOP   __ __ __ (__) __

3. ABTU   __ __ __ __

4. DMRSU   (__) __ __ __

5. EHLNOOPXY   __ __ __ __ __ __ __ __ (__)

6. ABCLMSY   (__) __ __ __ __ __

7. AGIRTU   __ __ __ __ __

8. EFLTU   __ __ (__) __ __

9. ACEILNRT   (__) __ __ __ __ __ __ __

10. AEHNOOPSX   __ __ __ __ __ __ __ __ __

Rearrange the letters written inside the circles above to make a word.

__ __ __ __ __ __ __ __

How many words can be made using the letters in the unscrambled word above? Write the words on the lines.

_____ _____ _____ _____

_____ _____ _____ _____

_____ _____ _____ _____

LETTER SORT #5

Directions: Rearrange each set of letters to name something you can read. Write the letters on the lines. Then, follow the directions below.

1. AAEGIMNZ __ __ __ __ __ __ __ (○)

2. AEENPPRSW __ __ __ __ __ __ __ (○)

3. AEILM __ - __ __ __ __

4. BKOOS __ (○) __ __

5. CEEIPRS (○) __ __ __ __ __ __

6. AMPS __ (○) __ __

7. EELRSTT __ (○) __ __ __ __ __

8. ACDIINORTY __ __ __ (○) __ __ __ __ __ __

9. GINSS (○) __ __ __ __

10. CDEIINORST __ (○) __ __ __ __ __ __ __ __

Rearrange the letters written inside the circles above to make a word.

__ __ __ __ __ __ __ __ __ __

How many words can be made using the letters in the unscrambled word above? Write the words on the lines.

_____ _____ _____ _____

_____ _____ _____ _____

_____ _____ _____ _____

LETTER SORT #6

Directions: Rearrange each set of letters to name something you look at. Write the letters on the lines. Then, follow the directions below.

1. CEIPRTU   __ __ __ ◯__ __

2. EEIILNOSTV   __ __ __ __ __ __ ◯__ __ __

3. IMNOORT   ◯__ __ __ __ __

4. AGHHOOPPRT   __ __ ◯__ __ __ __ __ __

5. AGIINNPT   __ ◯__ __ __ __ __

6. ALMRU   __ ◯__ __ __

7. ABEKOORY   __ __ ◯__ __ __ __ __

8. ABLMU   __ __ __ ◯__

9. EIVW   __ __ ◯__

10. ENSSTU   __ __ __ __ __ __

Rearrange the letters written inside the circles above to make a set of words.

— — —   — — — — — — —

How many words can be made using the letters in the unscrambled word above? Write the words on the lines.

_____   _____   _____   _____

_____   _____   _____   _____

_____   _____   _____   _____

LETTER SORT #7

Directions: Rearrange each set of letters to name things that move with the wind. Write the letters on the lines. Then, follow the directions below.

1. AFGLS   __ __◯__ __

2. ADLNRUY   __ __ __ __◯__ __

3. AEELSV   __ __ __ __ __ __

4. AEPPR   __ __ __ __ __

5. CEHIMS   __ __ __ __ __ __

6. AABILOSST __ __ __ __ __◯__ __ __

7. EIKST   __ __◯__ __

8. ABLLNOOS   __ __ __ __◯__ __ __

9. EERST   __◯__ __ __

10. DIILLMNSW __ __◯__ __ __ __ __ __

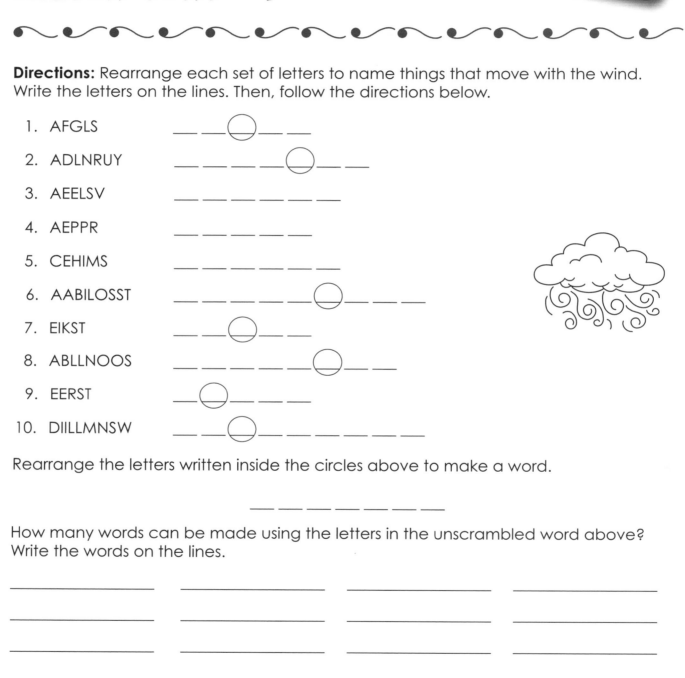

Rearrange the letters written inside the circles above to make a word.

__ __ __ __ __ __ __ __

How many words can be made using the letters in the unscrambled word above? Write the words on the lines.

_____   _____   _____   _____

_____   _____   _____   _____

_____   _____   _____   _____

LETTER SORT #8

Directions: Rearrange each set of letters to name a color. Write the letters on the lines. Then, follow the directions below.

1. ELLOWY   __ ◯ __ ◯ __ __

2. ACEEHRRSTU   __ __ __ __ __ __ __ __ __

3. EIOQRSTUU   __ __ __ __ __ __ __ ◯ __

4. AAAEIMNQRU   __ __ __ __ ◯ __ __ __ __

5. DGIINO   __ __ __ __ __ __

6. EILOTV   ◯ __ __ __ __ __

7. DGHIIMNT   __ ◯ __ __ __ __ __

8. IKMNPPU   __ __ __ __ __ __ __

9. ADGILMOR   __ ◯ __ __ __ __ __

10. AEINNS   __ __ ◯ __ __ __

Rearrange the letters written inside the circles above to make a word.

__ __ __ __ __ __ __ __

How many words can be made using the letters in the unscrambled word above? Write the words on the lines.

_____ _____ _____ _____

_____ _____ _____ _____

_____ _____ _____ _____

WORD BRIDGES #1

Directions: Circle the animal's name hidden in each sentence.

1. We do go to school every day.

2. If Roger is late, what can we do?

3. The dancers got dressed in the wardrobe area.

4. Sue came late to the party.

5. We will go at eight o'clock.

6. She never chews gum.

7. The ship *Pollyanna* is quite old.

8. How long did it last?

Play Word Play Word Play Word Play Word

WORD BRIDGES #2

Directions: Circle the name of a food hidden in each sentence.

1. Sal added the numbers.

2. Bob read the book.

3. Visit me at the zoo.

4. All I'm eating is a bun.

5. The busy bee told a story.

6. Peg got an A on the test.

7. The whales at the cape are huge!

8. The stuffed, little monster is cute.

WORD BRIDGES #3

Directions: Circle the name of a body part hidden in each sentence.

1. The monkey eats bananas.

2. The ad is in today's newspaper.

3. Frank needs a hair cut.

4. Purple glasses are cool!

5. The car made a turn.

6. Hannah and Conley are friends.

7. Sue's kin will visit her for the holidays.

8. Which ink is best?

WORD BRIDGES #4

Directions: Circle the number word hidden in each sentence.

1. The house vent is open.

2. He ate nuts and berries.

3. The ice froze Rose's toes.

4. We will go next week.

5. Dad left work at home.

6. The clarinet came with reeds.

7. Mrs. Smith left off our names.

8. If I've time, I can help you.

WORD BRIDGES #5

Directions: Circle the name of a fastener hidden in each sentence.

1. It's not the flu but tonsillitis!

2. Baby Chris naps every day.

3. My dog Zip performs cool tricks.

4. Ela sticks to her story.

5. First, ring the bell.

6. Peter opened the package.

7. When cooking, Mabel takes her time.

8. They will clap inside the theater.

WORD BRIDGES #6

Directions: Circle the names of items that are often round hidden in each sentence.

1. Race really fast to the next marker.

2. The camper brushed off ants.

3. What spices or ingredients are in the recipe?

4. Sabena woke up late because she was tired.

5. "Moo," Nellie the cow uttered.

6. Bow, heel, and stern are all boat terms.

7. Cassie is under the bridge.

8. Dominic locked the door.

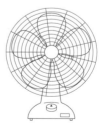

WORD BRIDGES #7

Directions: Circle the word related to dogs hidden in each sentence.

1. Bob rushed home.

2. Did you hear Susan sing?

3. The healed elbow looks great.

4. He said only to call "if urgent."

5. Greta illustrates children's books.

6. We can use a raffle as a fund-raiser.

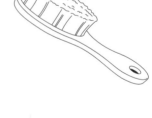

7. The tag said dry clean only.

8. Don't bar Kevin from the club.

WORD BRIDGES #8

Directions: Circle the name of an article of clothing hidden in each sentence.

1. We will sneak Ernie into the party.

2. What does the short sail on the boat do?

3. It is best to wash at night.

4. Rebecca put the lamp on the table.

5. He kneeled on the hassock so that he could rest.

6. Meg loves turkey.

7. We can admit ten students.

8. Carlos, we ate red apples.

BOWLING FOR LETTERS #1

Directions: Each player takes a turn to try to "bowl" a "strike" or a "spare." The object is to keep taking turns in order to spell out the longest word(s) using the letters given on the pins.

Strike: Using all 10 letters in one word	30 points
Spare: Using all 10 letters in two words	15 points
Other Points: Additional words	3 points each word

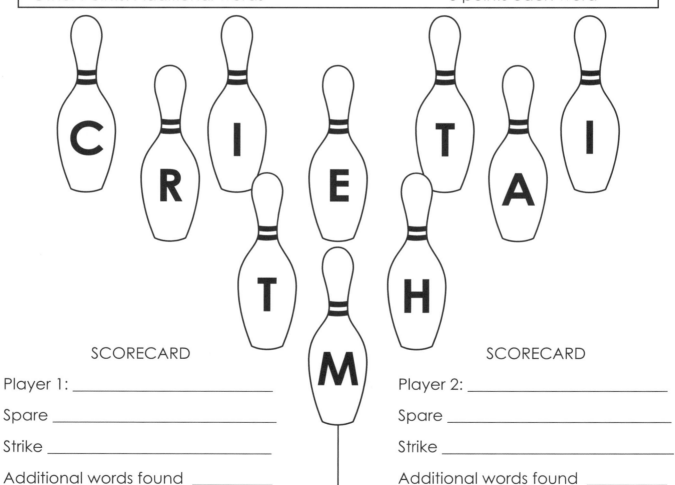

SCORECARD

Player 1: _____

Spare _____

Strike _____

Additional words found _____

_____

Total points: _____

SCORECARD

Player 2: _____

Spare _____

Strike _____

Additional words found _____

_____

Total points: _____

BOWLING FOR LETTERS #2

Directions: Each player takes a turn to try to "bowl" a "strike" or a "spare." The object is to keep taking turns in order to spell out the longest word(s) using the letters given on the pins.

Strike: Using all 10 letters in one word	30 points	
Spare: Using all 10 letters in two words	15 points	
Other Points: Additional words	3 points each word	

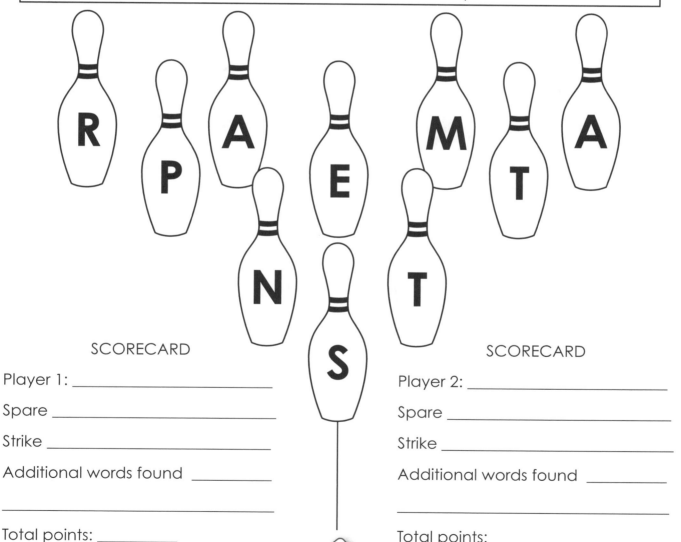

SCORECARD

Player 1: _____

Spare _____

Strike _____

Additional words found _____

_____

Total points: _____

SCORECARD

Player 2: _____

Spare _____

Strike _____

Additional words found _____

_____

Total points: _____

BOWLING FOR LETTERS #3

Directions: Each player takes a turn to try to "bowl" a "strike" or a "spare." The object is to keep taking turns in order to spell out the longest word(s) using the letters given on the pins.

Strike: Using all 10 letters in one word	30 points
Spare: Using all 10 letters in two words	15 points
Other Points: Additional words	3 points each word

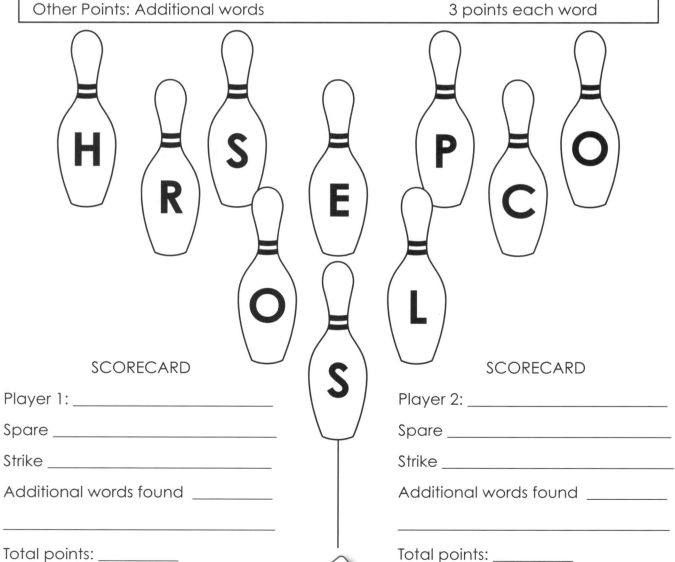

SCORECARD

Player 1: _____

Spare _____

Strike _____

Additional words found _____

_____

Total points: _____

SCORECARD

Player 2: _____

Spare _____

Strike _____

Additional words found _____

_____

Total points: _____

NAME_____   DATE_____

BOWLING FOR LETTERS #4

Directions: Each player takes a turn to try to "bowl" a "strike" or a "spare." The object is to keep taking turns in order to spell out the longest word(s) using the letters given on the pins.

Strike: Using all 10 letters in one word	30 points
Spare: Using all 10 letters in two words	15 points
Other Points: Additional words	3 points each word

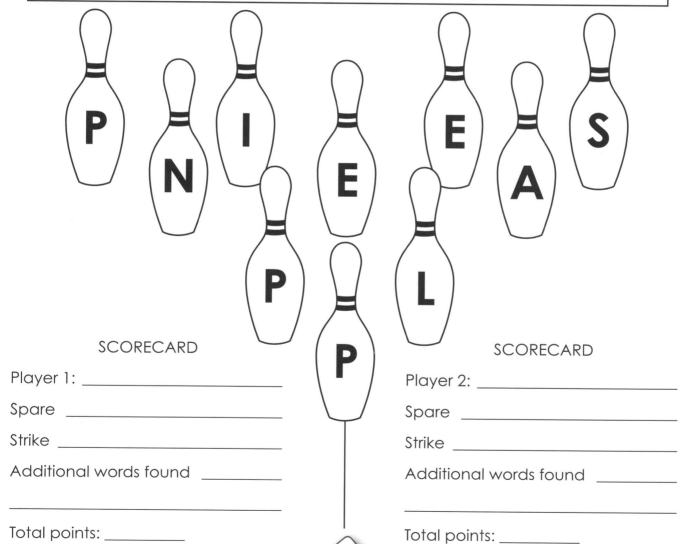

SCORECARD

Player 1: _____

Spare _____

Strike _____

Additional words found _____

_____

Total points: _____

SCORECARD

Player 2: _____

Spare _____

Strike _____

Additional words found _____

_____

Total points: _____

BOWLING FOR LETTERS #5

Directions: Each player takes a turn to try to "bowl" a "strike" or a "spare." The object is to keep taking turns in order to spell out the longest word(s) using the letters given on the pins.

Strike: Using all 10 letters in one word	30 points	
Spare: Using all 10 letters in two words	15 points	
Other Points: Additional words	3 points each word	

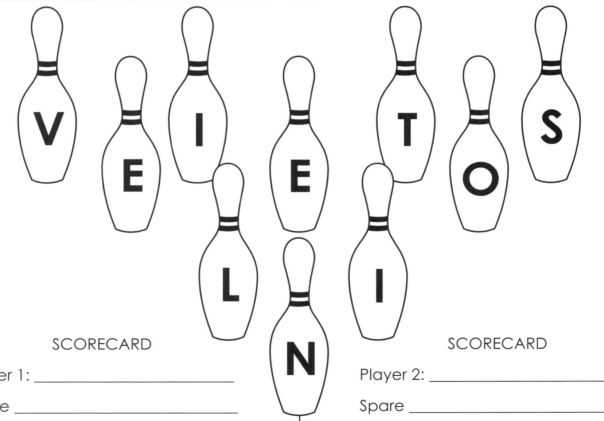

SCORECARD

Player 1: _____

Spare _____

Strike _____

Additional words found _____

_____

Total points: _____

SCORECARD

Player 2: _____

Spare _____

Strike _____

Additional words found _____

_____

Total points: _____

BOWLING FOR LETTERS #6

Directions: Each player takes a turn to try to "bowl" a "strike" or a "spare." The object is to keep taking turns in order to spell out the longest word(s) using the letters given on the pins.

Strike: Using all 10 letters in one word	30 points
Spare: Using all 10 letters in two words	15 points
Other Points: Additional words	3 points each word

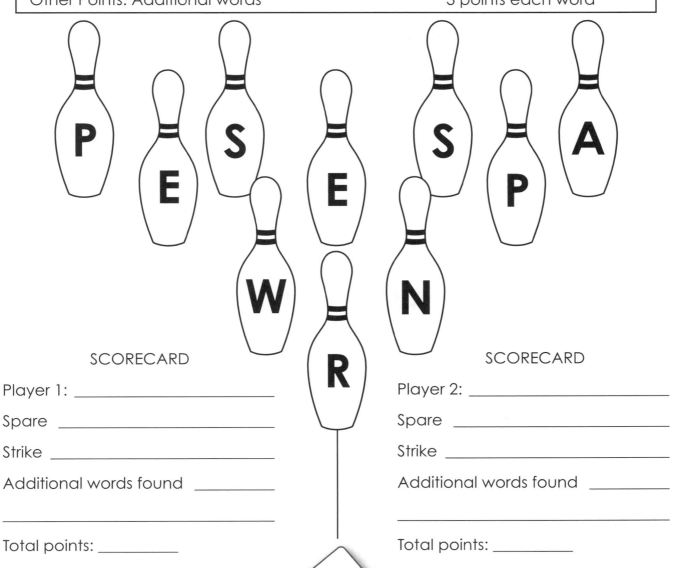

SCORECARD

Player 1: _____

Spare _____

Strike _____

Additional words found _____

_____

Total points: _____

SCORECARD

Player 2: _____

Spare _____

Strike _____

Additional words found _____

_____

Total points: _____

BOWLING FOR LETTERS #7

Directions: Each player takes a turn to try to "bowl" a "strike" or a "spare." The object is to keep taking turns in order to spell out the longest word(s) using the letters given on the pins.

Strike: Using all 10 letters in one word	30 points	
Spare: Using all 10 letters in two words	15 points	
Other Points: Additional words	3 points each word	

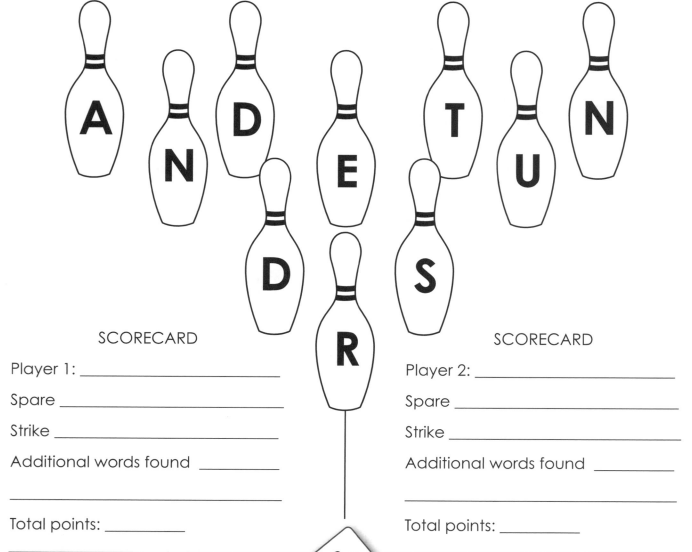

SCORECARD

Player 1: _____

Spare _____

Strike _____

Additional words found _____

_____

Total points: _____

SCORECARD

Player 2: _____

Spare _____

Strike _____

Additional words found _____

_____

Total points: _____

BOWLING FOR LETTERS #8

Directions: Each player takes a turn to try to "bowl" a "strike" or a "spare." The object is to keep taking turns in order to spell out the longest word(s) using the letters given on the pins.

Strike: Using all 10 letters in one word	30 points
Spare: Using all 10 letters in two words	15 points
Other Points: Additional words	3 points each word

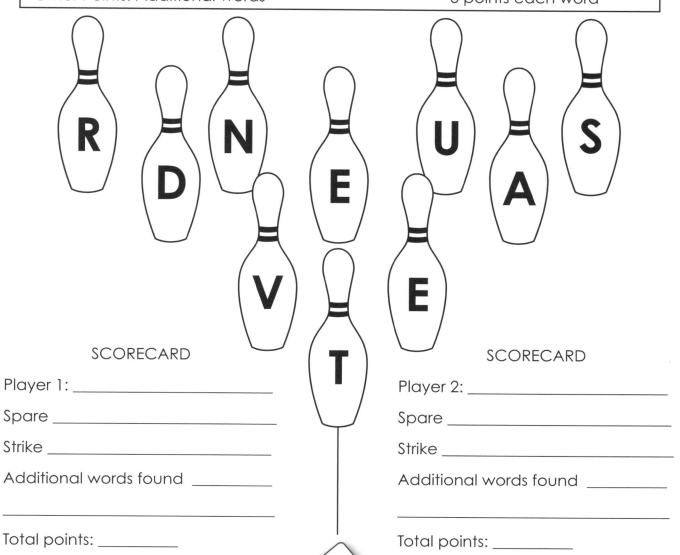

SCORECARD

Player 1: _____

Spare _____

Strike _____

Additional words found _____

_____

Total points: _____

SCORECARD

Player 2: _____

Spare _____

Strike _____

Additional words found _____

_____

Total points: _____

BOWLING FOR LETTERS #9

Directions: Each player takes a turn to try to "bowl" a "strike" or a "spare." The object is to keep taking turns in order to spell out the longest word(s) using the letters given on the pins.

Strike: Using all 10 letters in one word	30 points	
Spare: Using all 10 letters in two words	15 points	
Other Points: Additional words	3 points each word	

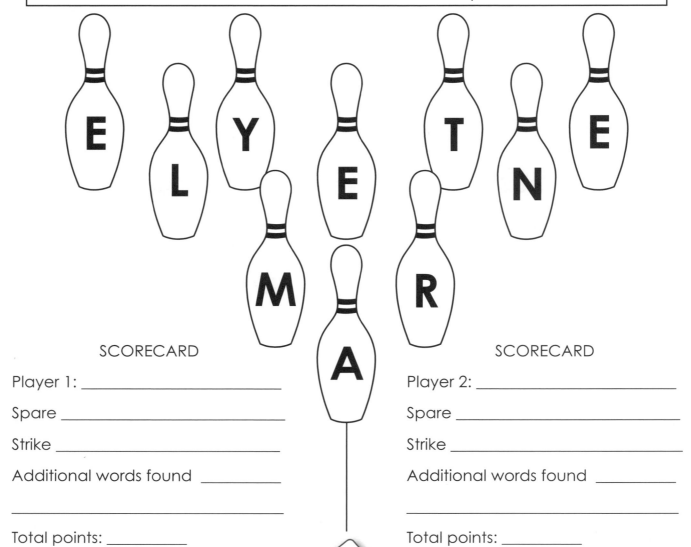

SCORECARD

Player 1: _____

Spare _____

Strike _____

Additional words found _____

_____

Total points: _____

SCORECARD

Player 2: _____

Spare _____

Strike _____

Additional words found _____

_____

Total points: _____

LEAP FROG #1

Directions: Start with the first pair of words on the first lily pad. Make the next word pair using the last word from the previous word pair as the first word for the next leap. Words that are made must be either compound words or "word buddies" (two words that are often used together). The goal is to reach the last pair of words on the last lily pad.

Word Bank									
ball	dragon	dragon	finger	finger	fly	fly	ring	snap	snap

Start here.

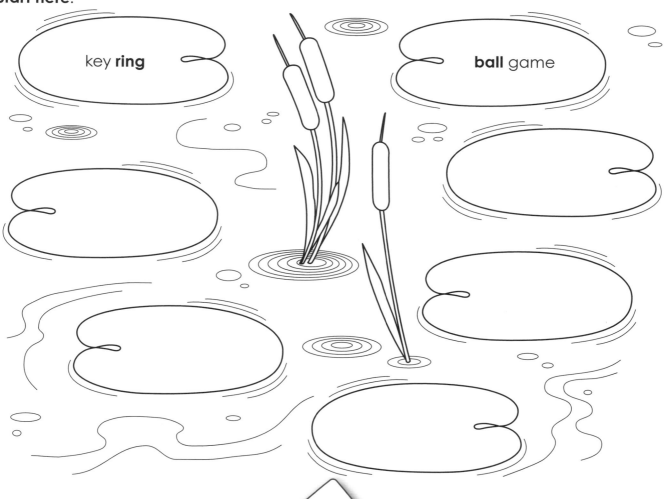

key **ring**

ball game

LEAP FROG #2

Directions: Start with the first pair of words on the first lily pad. Make the next word pair using the last word from the previous word pair as the first word for the next leap. Words that are made must be either compound words or "word buddies" (two words that are often used together). The goal is to reach the last word on the last lily pad.

Word Bank

ball   ball   camp   camp   day   fire   fire   fly   fly   room

Start here.

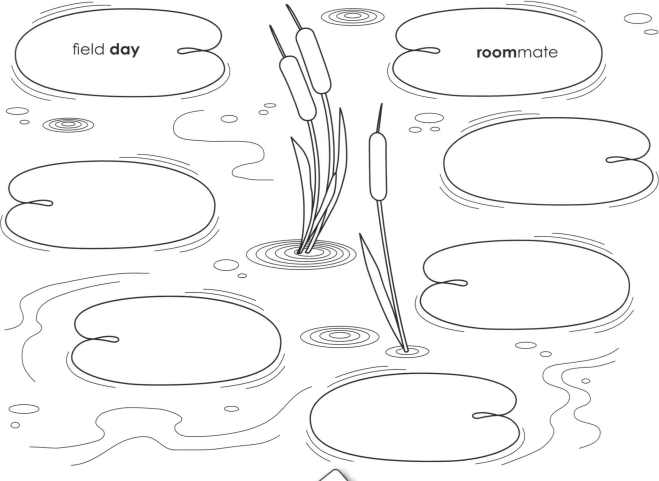

field **day**

roommate

102

LEAP FROG #3

Directions: Start with the first pair of words on the first lily pad. Make the next word using the last word from the previous word pair as the first word for the next leap. Words that are made must be either compound words or "word buddies" (two words that are often used together). The goal is to reach the last word on the last lily pad.

Word Bank									
bath	bath	bird	bird	blue	line	out	out	time	time

Start here.

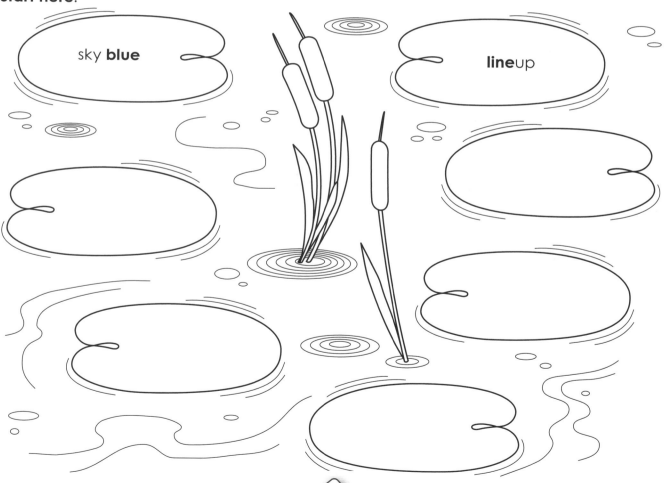

sky **blue**

lineup

LEAP FROG #4

Directions: Start with the first pair of words on the first lily pad. Make the next word using the last word from the previous word pair as the first word for the next leap. Words that are made must be either compound words or "word buddies" (two words that are often used together). The goal is to reach the last pair of words on the last lily pad.

Word Bank									
ball	ball	basket	basket	bread	bread	corn	corn	game	pop

Start here.

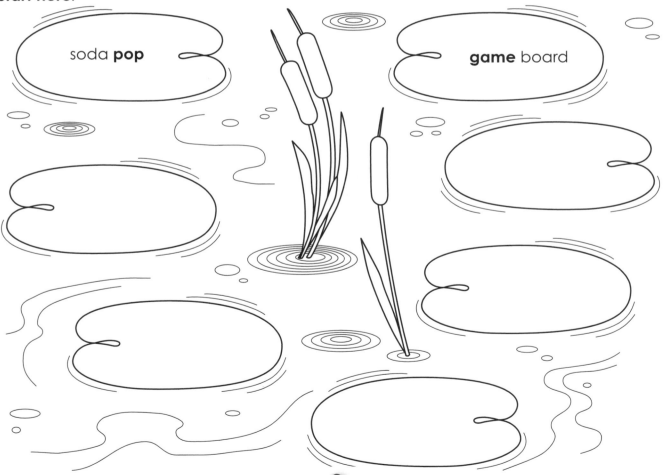

soda **pop**

game board

LEAP FROG #5

Directions: Start with the first pair of words on the first lily pad. Make the next word using the last word from the previous word pair as the first word for the next leap. Words that are made must be either compound words or "word buddies" (two words that are often used together). The goal is to reach the last pair of words on the last lily pad.

Word Bank
ball   ball   bench   fish   fish   park   park   star   stick   stick

Start here.

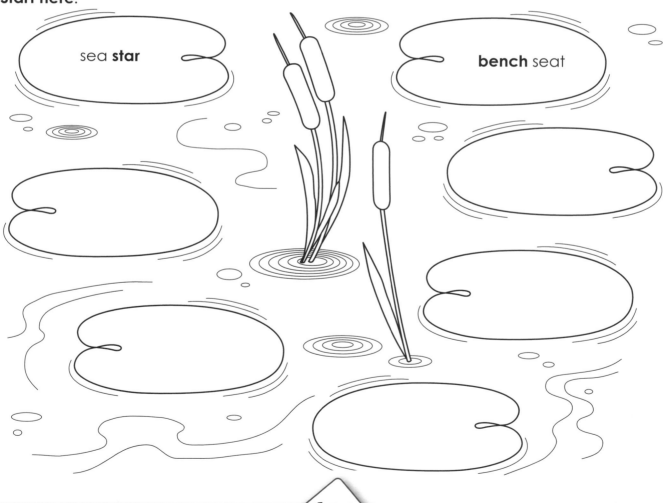

sea **star**

bench seat

LEAP FROG #6

Directions: Start with the word on the first lily pad. Make the next word using the last word from the previous word as the first word for the next leap. Words that are made must be either compound words or "word buddies" (two words that are often used together). The goal is to reach the last word on the last lily pad.

Word Bank									
back	back	door	door	hand	horse	horse	saw	saw	step

Start here.

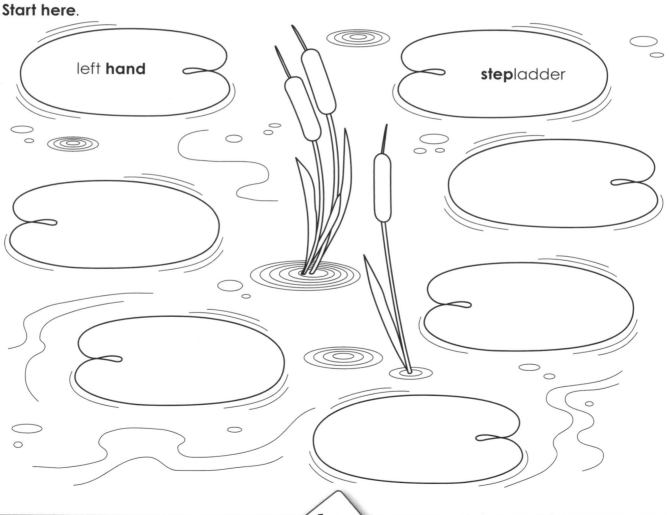

left **hand**

stepladder

LEAP FROG #7

Directions: Start with the first word on the first lily pad. Make the next word using the last word from the previous word as the first word for the next leap. Words that are made must be either compound words or "word buddies" (two words that are often used together). The goal is to reach the last word on the last lily pad.

Word Bank
box   box   lunch   lunch   mail   out   out   side   time   time

Start here.

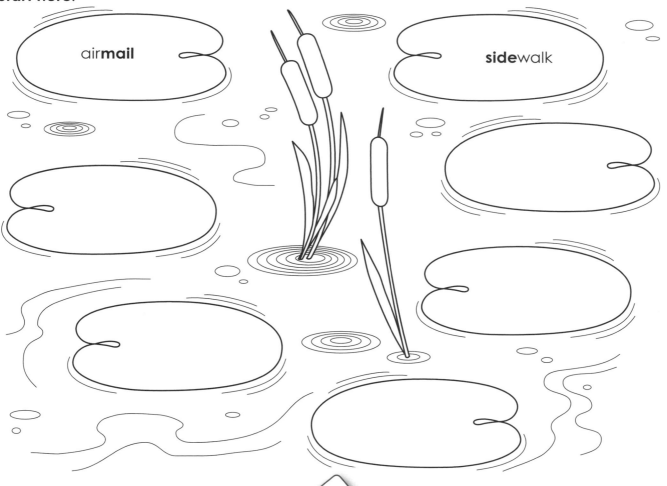

LOOK-ALIKES #1

Homographs are words that are spelled the same but have different meanings.

Example: A **bat** is a flying mammal.
            Who is next to **bat**?

| bridge | crow | dress | firm | pen |

Directions: Complete each pair of sentences with the correct homograph.

1. Put the baby in the play_____.

   Can I borrow your _____?

2. Do you like Mavis's wedding _____?

   What time should we _____ for dinner?

3. Every morning the rooster gives a loud _____.

   The black _____ likes to chase the cat.

4. Which law _____ does she work for?

   Is that a _____ offer?

5. The _____ spans the bay.

   Every Monday, my grandparents play _____ .

LOOK-ALIKES #2

Homographs are words that are spelled the same but have different meanings.

Example: A **bat** is a flying mammal.
Who is next to **bat**?

husky	kind	pupil	rash	tart

Directions: Complete each pair of sentences with the correct homograph.

1. Winnie is a _____ person.

   Which _____ of ice cream do you like?

2. The lemon wedge had a _____ flavor.

   My grandma made a delicious apple _____.

3. Jeremy is a _____ in room 412.

   The _____ is a part of the eye.

4. The _____ bear will stay warm this winter.

   A _____ is used to pull a sled.

5. The poison ivy gave Herbie a bad _____.

   Don't make a _____ decision.

LOOK-ALIKES #3

Homographs are words that are spelled the same but have different meanings.
      Example: A **bat** is a flying mammal.
                   Who is next to **bat**?

last	nap	second	will	yard

Directions: Complete each pair of sentences with the correct homograph.

1. He couldn't wait another _____.

   I am the _____ in line after Daisy.

2. The seamstress needs a _____ of fabric.

   Please mow the _____.

3. How long will this test _____?

   She was the _____ one to finish.

4. He has a very strong _____ to do his best.

   What _____ you make for dinner tonight?

5. The girl needs to take a _____.

   The _____ of the rug is fuzzy.

LOOK-ALIKES #4

Homographs are words that are spelled the same but have different meanings.

Example: A **bat** is a flying mammal.

Who is next to **bat**?

bass	batter	ear	flat	like

Directions: Complete each pair of sentences with the correct homograph.

1. My dad caught a _____ when he went fishing.

   Lila plays the double _____ in the orchestra.

2. Stir the cake _____ for one minute.

   Who is the next _____?

3. I _____ your outfit.

   He looks _____ he is getting sick.

4. The piece of wood is as _____ as a pancake.

   In Europe, an apartment is called a _____.

5. I ate the buttered _____ of corn.

   You should not stick anything in your _____.

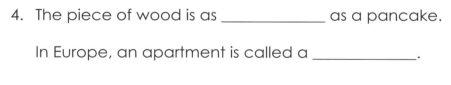

LOOK-ALIKES #5

Homographs are words that are spelled the same but have different meanings.

    Example: A **bat** is a flying mammal.
                      Who is next to **bat**?

blaze	gum	post	stalk	well

Directions: Complete each pair of sentences with the correct homograph.

1. I need to go to the _____ office.

   The _____ will support the fence.

2. Erica did _____ on the history test.

   How deep is the wishing _____?

3. The explorer set out to _____ a new trail.

   The _____ burned brightly.

4. Would you like a piece of bubble _____?

   His new braces sit just above his lower _____.

5. The cat will quietly _____ the mouse.

   Give me a _____ of celery, please.

LOOK-ALIKES #6

Homographs are words that are spelled the same but have different meanings.
        Example: A **bat** is a flying mammal.
                    Who is next to **bat**?

bank	box	duck	palm	row

Directions: Complete each pair of sentences with the correct homograph.

1. Jessica needs to _____ under the bars.

    What sound does a _____ make?

2. The bird took the seed from the _____ of my hand.

    _____ trees grow best in warm climates.

3. I need to go to the _____ on Main Street.

    The river_____ is full of rocks and pebbles.

4. Have you ever seen someone _____ in a ring?

    Will all of the books fit in that small _____?

5. How long did it take to _____ the boat?

    The farmer planted the beans in one long _____.

LOOK-ALIKES #7

Homographs are words that are spelled the same but have different meanings.
Example: A **bat** is a flying mammal.
Who is next to **bat**?

can	left	pound	sty	course

Directions: Complete each pair of sentences with the correct homograph.

1. I took a CPR _____ to prepare for baby-sitting.

    He finished the obstacle _____ in under five minutes.

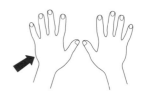

2. Do you write with your _____ hand?

    Who _____ the room first?

3. This room is a pig_____!

    Do you have a _____ on your eye?

4. Hand me a _____ of beans.

    When _____ we go to the lake?

5. It weighs about one _____.

    Please do not _____ on the door.

LOOK-ALIKES #8

Homographs are words that are spelled the same but have different meanings.

Example: A **bat** is a flying mammal.
                   Who is next to **bat**?

bear	clip	date	mole	spell

Directions: Complete each pair of sentences with the correct homograph.

1. He felt strange during the dizzy _____.

    How do you _____ this word?

2. I need a paper _____.

    _____ just a little bit of hair.

3. Have you ever eaten a _____?

    What is today's _____?

4. A _____ is a big animal.

    The weight was too much for her to _____.

5. She has a _____ on her back.

    A _____ likes to live underground.

LOOK-ALIKES #9

Homographs are words that are spelled the same but have different meanings.

    Example: A **bat** is a flying mammal.
                Who is next to **bat**?

| rest | story | tick | vault | yak |

Directions: Complete each pair of sentences with the correct homograph.

1. A _____ is an ox with long hair.

    Why does Erin _____ so much?

2. I need to take a short _____.

    What happened to the _____ of the pizza?

3. Can you hear the clock _____?

    I found a _____ on the dog.

4. The woman will _____ over the pole.

    Keep the money safe in the _____.

5. My mom works in a four- _____ building.

    Tell me a bedtime _____.

LOOK-ALIKES #10

Homographs are words that are spelled the same but have different meanings.

      Example: A **bat** is a flying mammal.

                     Who is next to **bat**?

cobbler	light	padded	pool	ring

Directions: Complete each pair of sentences with the correct homograph.

1. The _____ is filled with water.

   Do you know how to play _____?

2. The _____ is made of gold.

   Did you hear the bell _____?

3. The feather is very _____.

   It is becoming _____ outside.

4. Mom makes a great peach _____.

   The shoes need to be taken to the _____.

5. The dog _____ softly across the floor.

   James sat on the _____ chair.

STEPPING OUT

Directions: Starting at the bottom of each ladder, make a new word by adding a letter to each rung. The order of the letters cannot be changed.

1.

2.

3.

IN OTHER WORDS

Directions: Make as many words as you can using the letters from both words below.

_____   _____

1. _____   1. _____

2. _____   2. _____

3. _____   3. _____

4. _____   4. _____

5. _____   5. _____

6. _____   6. _____

7. _____   7. _____

8. _____   8. _____

9. _____   9. _____

10. _____   10. _____

11. _____   11. _____

12. _____   12. _____

LEAP FROG

Directions: Start with the first pair of words on the first lily pad. Make the next word or word pair using the last word from the previous word pair as the first word for the next leap. Words that are made must be either compound words or "word buddies" (two words that are often used together). The goal is to reach the last pair of words on the last lily pad.

Word Bank

Start here.

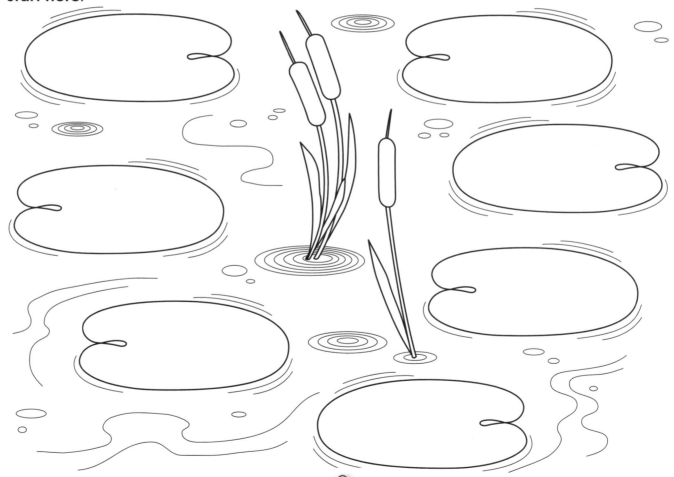

ANSWER KEY

Page 9
Sample answers
1. bed, bead
2. bet, best
3. bed, bred

Page 10
Sample answers
1. Ben, bean
2. men, omen
3. her, hear

Page 11
Sample answers
1. pin, spin
2. win, twin
3. fin, find

Page 12
Sample answers
1. win, wing
2. pit, pint
3. ton, tone

Page 13
Sample answers
1. for, four
2. for, fore
3. for, fort

Page 14
Sample answers
1. bus, bush
2. use, fuse
3. art, tart

Page 15
Sample answers
1. hat, heat, heart
2. has, hats, chats
3. ram, ream, dream

Page 16
Sample answers
1. his, hips, chips
2. ash, lash, slash
3. tin, thin, think

Page 17
1. horse
2. ball
3. fly
4. car
5. turtle
6. sand

Page 18
1. watch
2. bed
3. milk
4. chocolate
5. paper
6. candy

Page 19
1. bike
2. shoe
3. wheel
4. lion
5. party
6. mouse

Page 20
1. board
2. room
3. box
4. bus
5. lunch
6. work

Page 21
1. dog
2. butter
3. apple
4. stick
5. man
6. bean

Page 22
1. bottle
2. color
3. side
4. ball
5. pen
6. pie

Page 23
1. pan
2. cup
3. tree
4. fish
5. girl
6. pin

Page 24
1. light
2. truck
3. wash
4. tooth
5. bow
6. box

Page 25
1. dog
2. snake
3. frog
4. pig
5. sheep
6. hen

Page 26
1. spray
2. bird
3. monster
4. horse
5. shell
6. side

Page 27
1. RAN
2. OR
3. LAG
4. HER
5. FAT
6. LENT
7. TRICK
8. DENT
9. EAR
10. PEN
11. MEMO
12. LAB

Page 28
1. IF
2. ATE
3. TOW
4. ACE
5. AGE
6. HI
7. JAM
8. BE
9. ON
10. ANT
11. SO
12. OAT

Page 29
1. ICE
2. INK
3. REAM
4. SHE
5. SO
6. CUB
7. TEA
8. FRO
9. HOW
10. ACE
11. INK
12. NO

Page 30
1. HANG
2. HE
3. DOLL
4. BAN
5. DIM
6. PEN
7. CHAR
8. END
9. ART
10. IN
11. ONE
12. ALL

Page 31
1. KEY
2. TO
3. AN
4. ITCH
5. ILL
6. BOW
7. IN
8. IT
9. IT
10. PEN
11. ON
12. ATE

Page 32
1. ON
2. AM
3. USE
4. OR
5. GO
6. SHE
7. DO
8. LET
9. ROOST
10. TEN
11. LOB
12. IS

Page 33
1. ACT
2. CAME
3. DIRE
4. RIP
5. TAG
6. HEAR

Page 33 (cont.)
7. ON
8. MAN
9. VIE
10. HEAT
11. ICE
12. TICK

Page 34
1. EACH
2. DEN
3. OR
4. PAL
5. LAW
6. DENT
7. PORT
8. EDIT
9. RAM
10. RAN
11. ARCH
12. LOT

Page 35
gloves: gardening, driving, cotton
balls: basketball, beach, soccer
shoes: cleats, heels, slippers
race: human, horse, drag
nets: fishing, butterfly, hair
hats: cowboy, visor, top

Page 36
seabirds: albatross, pelican, seagull
poultry: chicken, turkey, duck
flightless: emu, ostrich, penguin
colorful: flamingo, peacock, toucan
feathers: down, plume, waterproof
feet: claws, talon, webbed

Page 37
homes: hut, tepee, castle
red: cherry, strawberry, stop sign
garden: spade, soil, vegetable
royalty: ruler, princess, queen
measure: foot, meter, mile
snow: ball, flake, man

Page 38
eye: cornea, iris, pupil
students: learners, classmates, peers
flowers: snapdragon, tulip, zinnia
glasses: goggles, spectacles, sun
pools: wading, swimming, car
twos: duo, pair, twins

Page 39
gold: bars, chain, mine
ring: telephone, toss, pinkie
blue: jeans, sky, moon
games: board, cards, trivia
puzzles: crossword, word search, jigsaw
beans: garbanzo, kidney, lima

Page 40
egg: cracked, scrambled, shell
pastry: Danish, strudel, puff
milk: chocolate, shake, whole
juice: apple, grape, orange
bread: white, garlic, rye
cereal: hot, rice, oatmeal

Page 41
paper: construction, notebook, wrapping
computer: keyboard, monitor, mouse
subjects: math, reading, science
lists: grocery, invitation, spelling
rodents: beaver, chipmunk, squirrel
things to read: book, newspaper, magazine

Page 42
things that hold: hands, folders, bottles
parts of a letter: address, name, greeting
collectibles: coins, cards, stamps
birthday items: confetti, wishes, gifts
head coverings: helmet, hood, wig
car parts: door, window, motor

Page 43
elephant
sample words: let, pant, pan, ant, pat, lent, lean, eat, leap, tea

hippopotamus
sample words: hip, pot, us, hot, hop, pop, Pam, hoot, is, it, hit

Page 44
hamburger
sample words: ham, urge, hug, am, age, bug, mug, hare, huge, burr, burger, her

pancakes
sample words: pan, cake, an, pace, ace, pane, cakes, paces, panes, aces, snap, snack

Page 45
computers
sample words: cop, cot, come, put, compute, mute, cots, cops, puts, mutes, cut, cuts, cute

reading
sample words: read, ad, ring, ding, red, din, in, ran, rag, rang, dear, raid

Page 46
decorate
sample words: dote, rate, rat, at, ate, date, core, or, oat, coat, crate, cot

presents
sample words: resent, resents, rent, rents, sent, preen, rest, rests, press, set, sets, pet, pets

Page 47
accordion
sample words: cord, an, Dan, in, ran, cod, con, coin, ad, accord, acorn, no, do, or, and, on, coo

Page 47 (cont.)
xylophone
sample words: lop, phone, one, on, loon, lone, lope, hoe

Page 48
Lincoln
sample words: in, inn, ill, Colin, no, on, coil, con, nil, oil, I, lion, coin

Washington
sample words: wash, ton, on, shin, sin, to, wag, was, wan, ash, as, at, a, I, in, tin, hit, no, not, hog, tag, nag, wing, ting, sing, sting, swing

Page 49
Australia
sample words: a, at, as, trail, rail, art, arts, rat, rats, Sal, salt, lit, sat, sit

North America
sample words: a, at, an, am, rot, torn, rice, race, came, ham, tame, ream, mire, or

Page 50
Mount Rushmore
sample words: rush, more, ore, or, rum, shore, sore, so, shoe, ruse, us, use, rue, hue, sue, moo, mesh, mush, she, sure, out

Mount Kilimanjaro
sample words: out, no, on, kilt, an, jam, Jan, kiln, not, nut, ran, milk, jar, join, man

Page 51
1. bass
2. base
3. lei
4. lay
5. loot
6. lute
7. stake

Page 51 (cont.)
8. steak
9. vary
10. very

Page 52
1. bazaar
2. bizarre
3. isle
4. aisle
5. build
6. billed
7. seem
8. seam
9. find
10. fined

Page 53
1. cells
2. sells
3. break
4. brake
5. site
6. sight
7. flair
8. flare
9. fare
10. fair

Page 54
1. toad, sheer
2. shear, towed
3. chews, cereal
4. serial, choose
5. guest, banned
6. guessed, band
7. male, allowed
8. mail, aloud
9. fowl, pier
10. peer, foul

Page 55
1. hear, gait
2. Here, gate
3. coupe, four
4. coop, for
5. vane, turn
6. tern, vain

Page 55 (cont.)
7. guest, cheep
8. guessed, cheap
9. bass, beat
10. beet, base

Page 56
1. herd, jam
2. heard, jamb
3. colonel, flu
4. kernel, flew
5. thrown, ball
6. bawl, throne
7. stare, plain
8. plane, stair
9. band, blew
10. blue, banned

Page 57
1. Aunt, Bea, two
2. to, ant, bee
3. I, ate, whole
4. eye, eight, hole
5. You, carat, dough
6. doe, ewe, carrot
7. knight, sail, sea
8. see, sale, night
9. won, knot, right
10. not, write, one

Page 58
1. son, sew, flower
2. so, flour, sun
3. Close, red, pail
4. read, pale, clothes
5. road, our, rose
6. hour, rode, rows
7. toe, weak, muscle
8. week, mussel, tow
9. naval, role, peace
10. Roll, piece, navel

Page 59
1. sent, tea, belle
2. cent, bell, tee
3. bear, hair, chili
4. hare, chilly, bare
5. pear, inn, Maine

Page 59 (cont.)
6. pair, in, main
7. ad, ewe, pain
8. You, add, pane
9. miner, to, know
10. minor, no, two

Page 60
1. balloon
2. van
3. subway
4. truck
5. station wagon
6. boat
7. gondola
8. motorcycle
9. train
10. walking
11. airplane
The secret message says: on a road trip

Page 61
1. Florida
2. Idaho
3. California
4. Utah
5. Wyoming
6. Louisiana
7. Washington
8. Kansas
9. Texas
10. Georgia
11. Kansas
The secret message says: fifty states

Page 62
1. cucumber
2. banana
3. tomato
4. fig
5. spinach
6. avocado
7. apple
8. carrot
9. date
10. grape

Page 62 (cont.)
11. cherry
The secret message says: Eat five a day.

Page 63
1. motion picture
2. candy
3. curtains
4. seats
5. ticket
6. laugh
7. excitement
8. project
9. movie
10. plot
11. screen
12. lobby
13. actors
14. action
The secret message says: Pass the popcorn.

Page 64
1. wolves
2. giraffes
3. snakes
4. hippos
5. parrots
6. jaguars
7. walruses
8. pandas
9. tigers
10. turtles
11. elephants
12. camels
13. zebras
14. owls
15. kangaroos
The secret message says: Visit us at the zoo.

Page 65
1. stitches
2. hospital
3. bed
4. flowers
5. thermometer

Page 65 (cont.)
6. medicine
7. paramedic
8. bandages
9. nurse
10. ambulance
11. cast
12. x-ray
13. surgery
14. doctor
15. gowns
16. instruments
The secret message says: the emergency room

Page 66
1. strawberry
2. coffee
3. banana
4. vanilla
5. swirl
6. butterscotch
7. chocolate
8. rocky road
9. lemon
10. candies
11. key lime
12. waffle cone
13. cookie dough
14. fudge royal
15. ice cream
16. mint
The secret message says: We all scream for it.

Page 67
1. solitaire
2. chess
3. tic-tac-toe
4. go fish
5. points
6. players
7. marbles
8. strategy
9. hopscotch
10. checkers
11. rules
12. goal
13. backgammon

Page 67 (cont.)
14. moves
15. amusement
16. sport
The secret message says: Let's play the games. (Apostrophe does not appear in puzzle.)

Page 68
1. Washington
2. Roosevelt
3. Lincoln
4. Hoover
5. Carter
6. Reagan
7. Clinton
8. Nixon

Page 69
1. reading
2. writing
3. arithmetic
4. history
5. spelling
6. science
7. orchestra
8. music

Page 70
1. volleyball
2. soccer
3. hockey
4. gymnastics
5. croquet
6. badminton
7. basketball
8. tennis

Page 71
1. Alabama
2. California
3. Hawaii
4. Alaska
5. Colorado
6. New York
7. Maryland
8. Wisconsin

Page 72
1. newspaper
2. magazine
3. diary
4. cereal box
5. letter
6. directions
7. recipe
8. message

Page 73
1. elephant
2. lion
3. rhinoceros
4. hippopotamus
5. orangutan
6. kangaroo
7. chameleon
8. camel

Page 74
1. teacher
2. principal
3. photographer
4. mechanic
5. carpenter
6. navigator
7. librarian
8. president

Page 75
1. folder
2. basket
3. container
4. bassinet
5. wagon
6. envelope
7. pockets
8. bucket

Page 76
1. English
2. spelling
3. writing
4. math
5. reading
6. science
7. music

Page 76 (cont.)
8. band
9. orchestra
10. library
Word: student
Sample words: dent, tent, nest, tune, den, set, dust, dune, sent, use, nuts, sue

Page 77
1. broccoli
2. leaves
3. frogs
4. grass
5. limes
6. lizards
7. alligators
8. clover
9. celery
10. emeralds
Word: forests
Sample words: fore, for, so, to, frost, rest, store, sore, tore, soft, sort, sorts

Page 78
1. French
2. German
3. English
4. Spanish
5. Russian
6. Chinese
7. Japanese
8. Korean
9. Swahili
10. Dutch
Word: people
Sample words: pope, pop, lop, lope, peep, pole, plop, peel, pep, Lee, Leo, eel, ole

Page 79
1. violin
2. piano
3. tuba
4. drums
5. xylophone
6. cymbals

Page 79 (cont.)
7. guitar
8. flute
9. clarinet
10. saxophone
Word: concert
Sample words: on, or, tone, ten, ton, to, cone, rent, not, toe, note, once

Page 80
1. magazine
2. newspaper
3. E-mail
4. books
5. recipes
6. maps
7. letters
8. dictionary
9. signs
10. directions
Word: reporters
Sample words: report, port, pot, post, to, so, or, pore, rose, rote, store, tore

Page 81
1. picture
2. television
3. monitor
4. photograph
5. painting
6. mural
7. yearbook
8. album
9. view
10. sunset
Word: art museum
Sample words: muse, use, me, sum, mum, us, mums, sue, mar, arm, ruse, meat, mute, smart, mart, mat, mast

Page 82
1. flags
2. laundry
3. leaves
4. paper

Page 82 (cont.)
5. chimes
6. sailboats
7. kites
8. balloons
9. trees
10. windmills
Word: tornado
Sample words: or, on, to, not, ton, too, do, door, and, ant, ran, rot

Page 83
1. yellow
2. chartreuse
3. turquoise
4. aquamarine
5. indigo
6. violet
7. midnight
8. pumpkin
9. marigold
10. sienna
Word: lavender
Sample words: lean, lane, den, end, vend, dear, deal, real, read, red, dean, need

Page 84
1. dog (do go)
2. frog (If Roger)
3. bear (wardrobe area)
4. camel (came late)
5. goat (go at)
6. hen (she never)
7. hippo (ship Pollyanna)
8. owl (how long)

Page 85
1. salad (Sal added)
2. bread (Bob read)
3. meat (me at)
4. lime (All I'm eating)
5. beet (bee told)
6. egg (Peg got)
7. pear (cape are)
8. lemon (little monster)

Page 86
1. eye (monkey eats)
2. head (The ad)

Page 86 (cont.)
3. knee (Frank needs)
4. leg (Purple glasses)
5. arm (car made)
6. hand (Hannah and)
7. skin (Sue's kin)
8. chin (Which ink)

Page 87
1. seven (house vent)
2. ten (ate nuts)
3. zero (froze Rose's)
4. one (go next)
5. two (left work)
6. three (with reeds)
7. four (off our)
8. five (If I've)

Page 88
1. button (but tonsillitis)
2. snaps (Chris naps)
3. zipper (Zip performs)
4. elastic (Ela sticks)
5. string (First, ring)
6. rope (Peter opened)
7. belt (Mabel takes)
8. pin (clap inside)

Page 89
1. cereal (Race really)
2. fan (off ants)
3. ring (or ingredients)
4. plate (up late)
5. moon ("Moo," Nellie)
6. wheel (bow, heel)
7. sun (is under)
8. clock (Dominic locked)

Page 90
1. brush (Bob rushed)
2. ears (hear Susan)
3. bowl (elbow looks)
4. fur (if urgent)
5. tail (Greta illustrates)
6. fleas (raffle as)
7. tags (tag said)
8. bark (bar Kevin)

Page 91
1. sneaker (sneak Ernie)
2. shorts (short sail)
3. hat (wash at)
4. cap (Rebecca put)
5. socks (hassock so)
6. gloves (Meg loves)
7. mitten (admit ten)
8. sweater (Carlos, we ate red)

Page 92
Strike: arithmetic
Sample Spare: chime, trait
Sample Additional Words Found: hit, mire, tire, hire, tame, meat, rice

Page 93
Strike: apartments
Sample Spare: parts, meant
Sample Additional Words Found: team, meat, met, mat, map, maps, rent, reap

Page 94
Strike: preschools
Sample Spare: chore, slops
Sample Additional Words Found: pores, slope, pole, rose, hose, sole

Page 95
Strike: pineapples
Sample Spare: pine, apples
Sample Additional Words Found: peel, pail, seen, lane, lap, line, sap, pin

Page 96
Strike: television
Sample Spare: stein
Sample Additional Words Found: ties, violet, seen, tine, vein, toes

Page 97
Strike: newspapers
Sample Spare: news, papers
Sample Additional Words Found: pears, wear, near, seen, pen, pan, sew, seep

Page 98
Strike: understand
Sample Spare: under, stand
Sample Additional Words Found:
and, sand, ruse, rant, use, dare, tan, sad

Page 99
Strike: adventures
Sample Spare: advent, sure
Sample Additional Words Found:
vat, vent, rent, nut, net, veer, vet, rats

Page 100
Strike: elementary
Sample Spare: element, ray
Sample Additional Words Found:
lay, meant, rent, year, mere, near, net, met

Page 101
ring finger
finger snap
snapdragon
dragonfly
fly ball

Page 102
day camp
campfire
firefly
fly ball
ballroom

Page 103
bluebird
birdbath
bath time
time-out
outline

Page 104
popcorn
corn bread
breadbasket
basketball
ball game

Page 105
starfish
fish stick
stickball
ballpark
park bench

Page 106
handsaw
sawhorse
horseback
backdoor
doorstep

Page 107
mailbox
box lunch
lunchtime
time-out
outside

Page 108
1. pen
2. dress
3. crow
4. firm
5. bridge

Page 109
1. kind
2. tart
3. pupil
4. husky
5. rash

Page 110
1. second
2. yard
3. last
4. will
5. nap

Page 111
1. bass
2. batter
3. like
4. flat
5. ear

Page 112
1. post
2. well
3. blaze
4. gum
5. stalk

Page 113
1. duck
2. palm
3. bank
4. box
5. row

Page 114
1. course
2. left
3. sty
4. can
5. pound

Page 115
1. spell
2. clip
3. date
4. bear
5. mole

Page 116
1. yak
2. rest
3. tick
4. vault
5. story

Page 117
1. pool
2. ring
3. light
4. cobbler
5. padded